HORSE PACKING IN PICTURES

To Mike
All best wishes
and many happy trails
Francis W. Davis

HORSE PACKING IN PICTURES

SECOND EDITION

Francis W. Davis

HOWELL BOOK HOUSE

New York

Collier Macmillan Canada
Toronto

Maxwell Macmillan International
New York   Oxford   Singapore   Sydney

Howell Book House
Macmillan Publishing Company
866 Third Avenue
New York, NY 10022

Collier Macmillan Canada, Inc.
1200 Eglinton Avenue East, Suite 200
Don Mills, Ontario M3C 3N1

Library of Congress Cataloging-in-Publication Data

Davis, Francis W.
    Horse packing in pictures / Francis W. Davis. — 2nd ed.
      p.   cm.
    ISBN 0-87605-899-3
    1. Packhorse camping. I. Title.
    GV199.7.D38 1991   90-22266   CIP
    796.54—dc20

Macmillan books are available at special discounts for bulk
purchases for sales promotions, premiums, fund-raising, or
educational use. For details, contact:

Special Sales Director
Macmillan Publishing Company
866 Third Avenue
New York, NY 10022

10 9 8 7 6 5 4 3 2 1

Printed in the United States of America

With fondest memories of a dear friend,

CAPTAIN SAMUEL A. HENDRICKSON,

and the members of his beloved 10th Mountain Division

with which he served during World War II.

ACKNOWLEDGMENTS

My sincerest thanks go to the following people whose kind help and encouragement have meant so much to me through all the months it took to put this book together.

Blanche H. Davis, my wife, who at the time of the first publication was the widow of Captain Samuel A. Hendrickson and surviving owner of the 5-H Acres School of Riding in Cortland, New York; it was at the urging of Dolly, as she is affectionately known, that *Horse Packing in Pictures* was begun, and her generous cooperation accompanied it to its completion;

Andrew D. Hastings, Jr., Historian/Archivist, National Association of the 10th Mountain Division, Inc., who made available a copy of a War Department field manual on pack transportation;

Susan Harris, former director, and *Linda Minard*, former instructor at 5-H Acres at the time of first publication, who so patiently endured my forever being under foot with packing equipment and my borrowing horses and students for photos or to try out new ideas;

Anna Watson and *Louis Plagge*, former students at 5-H Acres, who spent countless hours packing and unpacking horses and posing while I shot film after film to work from;

Dr. Sam Sabin, professor at Cornell University, Ithaca, New York, and Extension Horse Specialist in charge of the 4-H Horse Program in New York State; his wonderful enthusiasm and help with 4-H horse packing and other projects has had an important bearing on this book;

Laurie Graham, the editor of the first edition, for her patience and understanding while I went off on pack trips that delayed completion of the drawings, and for being from Big Horn, Wyoming, and knowing about horse packing;

Dick Ereaux of Mission Valley Saddlery, Ronan, Montana, for the detailed information on his beautiful decker pack saddle, panniers, and accessories shown on page 38;

P. R. Van Scoyk of the Colorado Saddlery Co., Denver, Colorado, for information on the canvas saddle panniers on page 39;

Joe B. Johnson, Extension Livestock Specialist, Washington State University, who so thoughtfully sent along information on manteeing and hitches;

Dr. S. E. Deal of I-Deal Ideas, Inc., Polson, Montana, for information on "Coolback" pack saddle pad and accessories, page 35;

Guy Johannes, Jr. who, when we first met in 1969, had organized an outdoor association, nicknamed the "O. A." among students at Western New Mexico University in Silver City, where he held an assistant professorship. Guy's dreams of acquainting young people with nature via the pack train were a great inspiration to me. I consider myself most fortunate to have acquired his assistance as consultant and proofreader.

The list of credits would not be complete without a word of appreciation for 5-H Acres' incomparable Albert, without a doubt the most patient and good humored horse-of-all-trades anywhere. He took to packing like a duck to water.

CONTENTS

FOREWORD

During what now rapidly approaches a half century of working with horses and horsemen, it has been my fortune to have met quite a number of people who were professional horsemen and horsewomen in the truest sense. Yet only rarely have I encountered a person like Francis Davis, a man who has a deep insight and a real appreciation of the beautiful harmony that can exist among man, horses, and nature.

There have been more than ten thousand books dealing with horses and their use published in the English language. Only a few of these have become classics. Mr. Davis's book is surely destined to become one of them. This book is authoritative without being pompous. It is thorough without being burdened with tedious repetition and insignificant detail. The illustrations are magnificent; each is not only a work of art, but a story unto itself. Much of this book represents knowledge gained by many people over the years, carefully selected and sorted. Yet some of this book is unique, the material developed by a man with an inquisitive nature and a very practical bent.

The real value of this book cannot be appreciated immediately even by those who have a great deal of experience with packing. Little things, small details which easily could have been overlooked, seem to emerge from every page. So for the experienced packer there is much that is new and much to be learned. For the beginner, this book shows a new and exciting way to enjoy a horse, the environment, and, yes, even an association with one's fellow men.

I hope the reader of this book will experience through its words and pictures some of the excitement and enthusiasm of the artist-author—enthusiasm not only for packing, but also for the opportunities which packing provides. To say more would be easy but superfluous. This book speaks for itself.

Dr. Samuel W. Sabin, Professor
of Animal Science, Cornell University,
and 4-H Horse Specialist

PREFACE

In times long past, many kinds of activity in the back country were kept alive and healthy by packers and strings of horses or mules which were the lifelines to the outside world. Things have changed a great deal since then, but the reliable old pack string still plays an important role as more and more hunters, fishermen, nature lovers and just plain civilization-scarred escapees from the "Good Life" pick up a lead rope and follow a guide into what's left of the wilderness that man likes to think of as *his* heritage.

Horse pack trips are also one of the most interesting and rewarding activities open to horse enthusiasts. Backyard riding, bridle trails, and horse shows are fine, but a pack trip into the wilderness can spice up the old menu with a helping of honest-to-goodness adventure and a shot at the unknown.

Like any activity involving the temperaments of several individuals, be they men or beasts, horse pack trips must be carefully planned and executed to insure success. Trusting souls who venture into the wilderness via horse and pack without the necessary knowledge and preparation can come out much the worse for wear. Consider the sight of belongings, poorly packed, strewn along a mountain trail as a horse, frightened out of his wits by a flapping tarp, tries to outrun it to the horizon. What's even more distressing is how long the walk back can seem after all the horses, having been improperly secured, have departed for home and are ten miles ahead on the trail.

Among the lessons which can best be learned by living for a while in the wilderness is that man's artificial environment does not supply the needs of his existence but that in fact his extravagant life style and everything he has are possible only because of a world that was once all wilderness.

This vast storehouse of life-sponsoring supplies which we call *our* natural resources has all too often been thought of as some sort of foe to be conquered. Actually wild country is a fragile thing and everyone who ventures into it carries with him the seeds of its destruction. We must tread softly when we visit the wilderness and leave it as clean and as beautiful as we found it. For that matter we might even try to improve it, not by rearranging things that are natural, but by picking up a paper, can, or bottle that someone has left behind.

I hope that this book will introduce an exciting experience to those new to horse packing and will rekindle for "old hands" memories of many wilderness trips in the good company of horses and other riders.

Who knows, with a little luck some day our paths may cross and we can share a campfire on the far side of a mountain overlooking an alpine meadow or lake and be able to relax, discuss the day's ride, and enjoy the music of Swiss bells that tells us our horses are grazing and all is well in the cool of the evening.

HORSE PACKING IN PICTURES

SELECTING A PACK HORSE—
GOOD ANIMAL

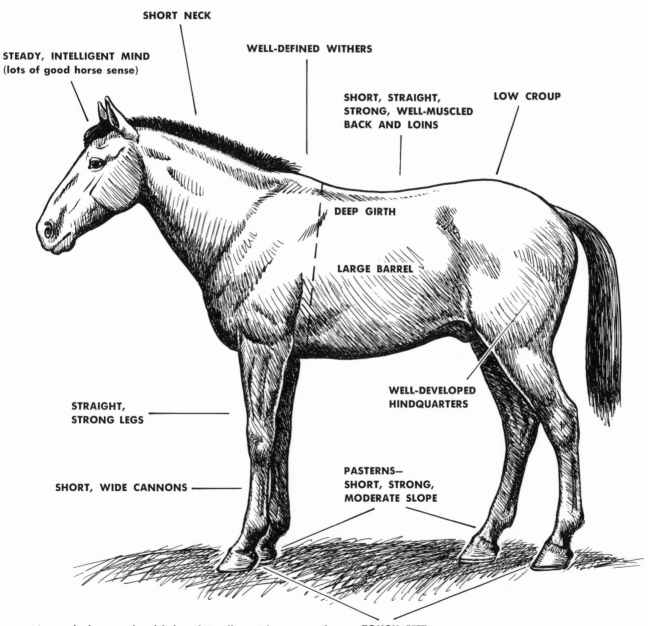

SHORT NECK

STEADY, INTELLIGENT MIND
(lots of good horse sense)

WELL-DEFINED WITHERS

SHORT, STRAIGHT,
STRONG, WELL-MUSCLED
BACK AND LOINS

LOW CROUP

DEEP GIRTH

LARGE BARREL

WELL-DEVELOPED
HINDQUARTERS

STRAIGHT,
STRONG LEGS

SHORT, WIDE CANNONS

PASTERNS—
SHORT, STRONG,
MODERATE SLOPE

TOUGH FEET
IN PROPORTION TO SIZE
AND WEIGHT OF HORSE

A pack horse should be friendly with a gentle
nature, have no fear of humans, be able and willing
to move out freely under pack, even on reasonably
rough-going trails, and should be sure-footed with
a minimum of rock and roll.

SELECTING A PACK HORSE—
GOOD POINTS

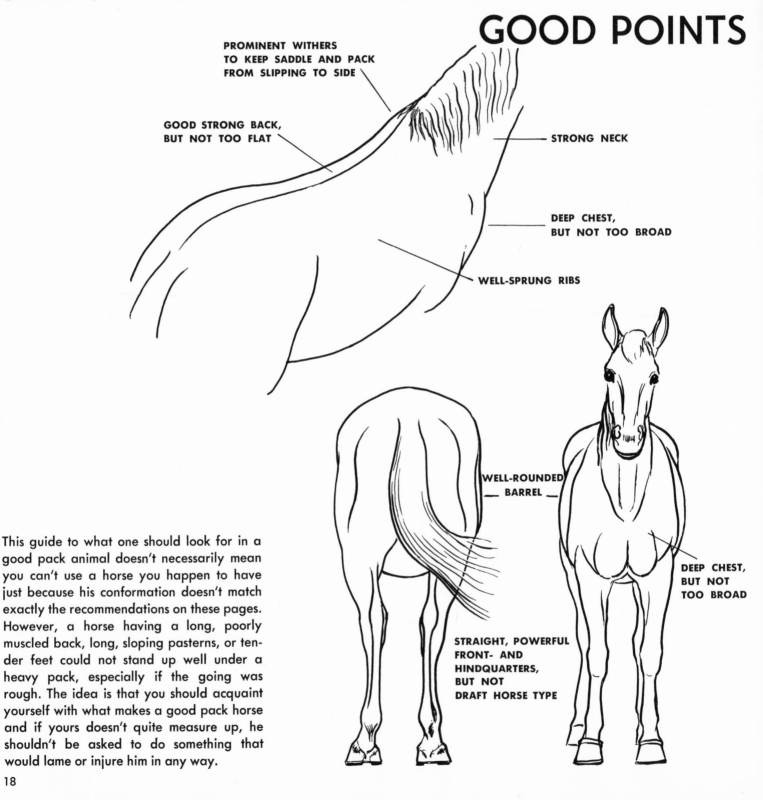

PROMINENT WITHERS
TO KEEP SADDLE AND PACK
FROM SLIPPING TO SIDE

GOOD STRONG BACK,
BUT NOT TOO FLAT

STRONG NECK

DEEP CHEST,
BUT NOT TOO BROAD

WELL-SPRUNG RIBS

WELL-ROUNDED
BARREL

DEEP CHEST,
BUT NOT
TOO BROAD

STRAIGHT, POWERFUL
FRONT- AND
HINDQUARTERS,
BUT NOT
DRAFT HORSE TYPE

This guide to what one should look for in a good pack animal doesn't necessarily mean you can't use a horse you happen to have just because his conformation doesn't match exactly the recommendations on these pages. However, a horse having a long, poorly muscled back, long, sloping pasterns, or tender feet could not stand up well under a heavy pack, especially if the going was rough. The idea is that you should acquaint yourself with what makes a good pack horse and if yours doesn't quite measure up, he shouldn't be asked to do something that would lame or injure him in any way.

18

SELECTING A PACK HORSE— POOR PACK TYPE

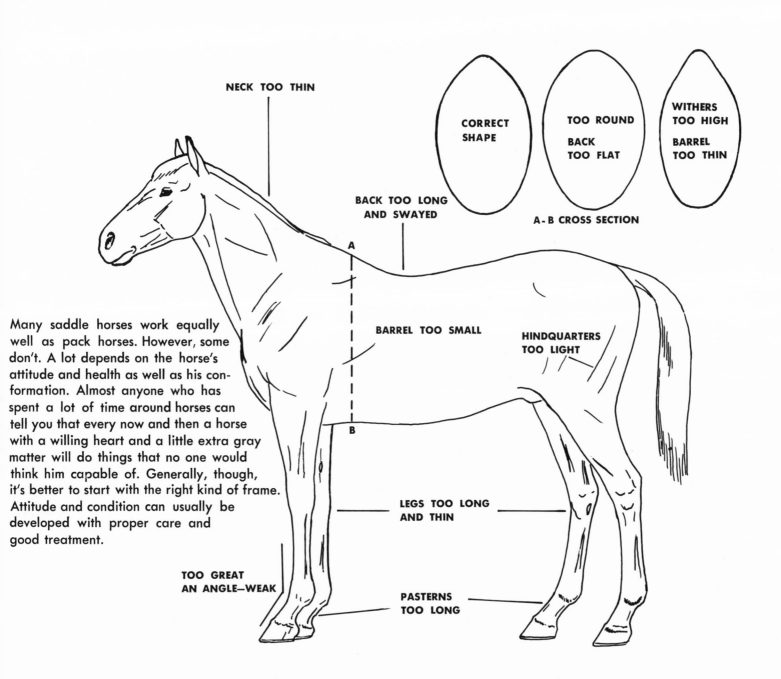

NECK TOO THIN

BACK TOO LONG AND SWAYED

CORRECT SHAPE

TOO ROUND
BACK TOO FLAT

WITHERS TOO HIGH
BARREL TOO THIN

A- B CROSS SECTION

A

BARREL TOO SMALL

HINDQUARTERS TOO LIGHT

B

Many saddle horses work equally well as pack horses. However, some don't. A lot depends on the horse's attitude and health as well as his conformation. Almost anyone who has spent a lot of time around horses can tell you that every now and then a horse with a willing heart and a little extra gray matter will do things that no one would think him capable of. Generally, though, it's better to start with the right kind of frame. Attitude and condition can usually be developed with proper care and good treatment.

LEGS TOO LONG AND THIN

TOO GREAT AN ANGLE—WEAK

PASTERNS TOO LONG

SELECTING A PACK HORSE—DEFECTS

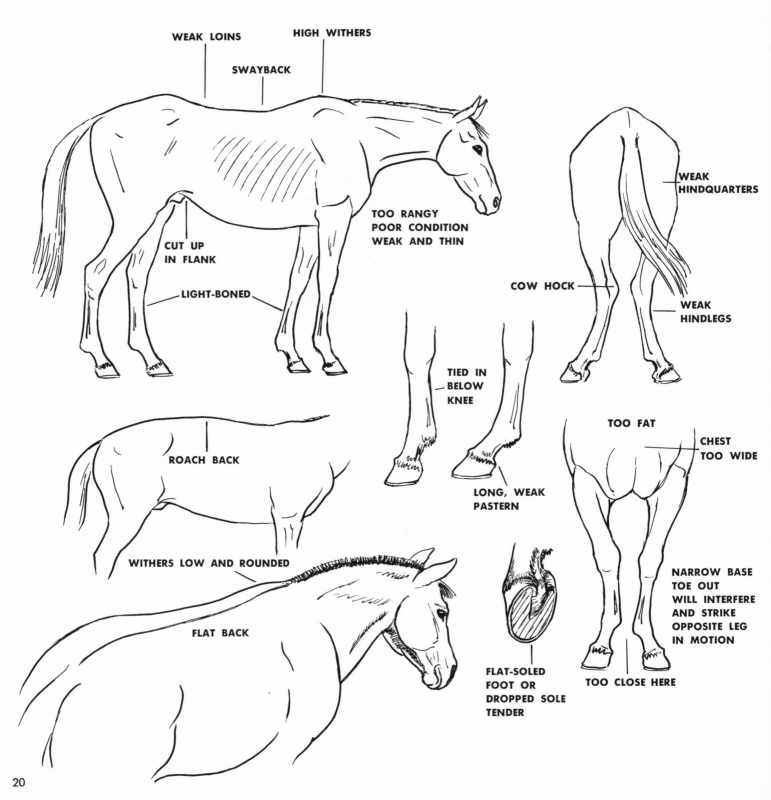

WEAK LOINS

HIGH WITHERS

SWAYBACK

TOO RANGY
POOR CONDITION
WEAK AND THIN

CUT UP
IN FLANK

LIGHT-BONED

WEAK
HINDQUARTERS

COW HOCK

WEAK
HINDLEGS

TIED IN
BELOW
KNEE

TOO FAT

CHEST
TOO WIDE

ROACH BACK

LONG, WEAK
PASTERN

WITHERS LOW AND ROUNDED

NARROW BASE
TOE OUT
WILL INTERFERE
AND STRIKE
OPPOSITE LEG
IN MOTION

FLAT BACK

FLAT-SOLED
FOOT OR
DROPPED SOLE
TENDER

TOO CLOSE HERE

SELECTING A PACK HORSE–INJURIES

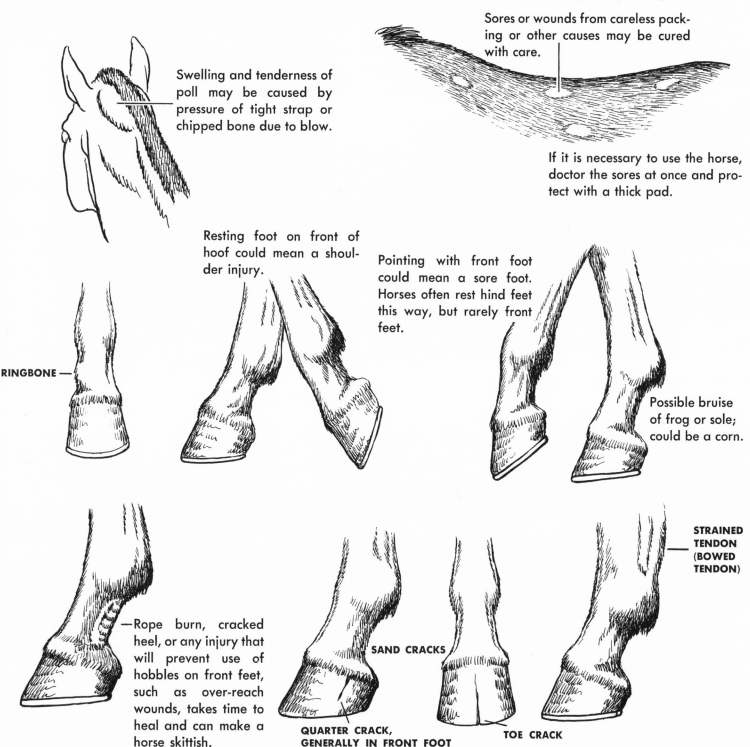

Swelling and tenderness of poll may be caused by pressure of tight strap or chipped bone due to blow.

Sores or wounds from careless packing or other causes may be cured with care.

If it is necessary to use the horse, doctor the sores at once and protect with a thick pad.

Resting foot on front of hoof could mean a shoulder injury.

Pointing with front foot could mean a sore foot. Horses often rest hind feet this way, but rarely front feet.

RINGBONE —

Possible bruise of frog or sole; could be a corn.

—Rope burn, cracked heel, or any injury that will prevent use of hobbles on front feet, such as over-reach wounds, takes time to heal and can make a horse skittish.

SAND CRACKS

STRAINED TENDON (BOWED TENDON)

QUARTER CRACK, GENERALLY IN FRONT FOOT

TOE CRACK

TRAINING THE PACK HORSE

You'll need a strong halter and a 10' to 12' lead, preferably with a swivel snap.

LEATHER OR NYLON WEBBING HALTER

GOOD IDEA

SHEEPSKIN NOSE BAND COVER

POLY ROPE HALTER

Start training with one horse at a time by leading him along trails and through wooded areas. Teach him to follow your horse through tight places and over obstacles.

GLOVES

After they pass the first grade, on to higher education—"tailing."

When they have learned that each horse must follow its leader around all obstacles, go through it again with a pack saddle and hay bales. Mantee bales to discourage snacking along the way.

TRAINING THE PACK HORSE

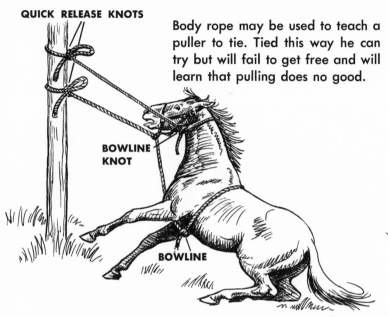

QUICK RELEASE KNOTS

BOWLINE KNOT

BOWLINE

Body rope may be used to teach a puller to tie. Tied this way he can try but will fail to get free and will learn that pulling does no good.

Eventually he will be cured of the pulling habit and will stand with any rope.

Teach your pack horse to stop when his lead rope is down.

Run lead rope through ground ring to hobbles. Repeat this until he stands when lead is dropped.

It could save you a lot of chasing if the weak link breaks or lead comes undone.

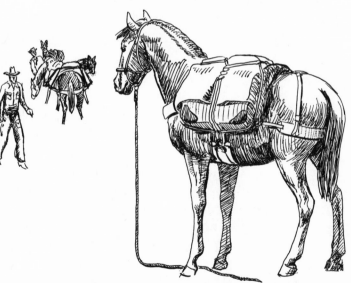

Practicing this and rewarding your horse when he stands will pay off someday when the real thing happens.

TRAINING THE PACK HORSE

Use swivel here to prevent this kind of damage to rope.

Without a swivel, if the horse keeps turning to the right long enough, strands will become unwound and separate.

To break a horse to a picket, use a large soft rope. Give him lots of open space—he'll work it out.

SWIVEL

Stone can also be used as drag.

To prevent a horse from becoming tangled in a narrow rope, slip a piece of old garden hose over it between swivel and drag. Hose makes it impossible to get a small loop around anything.

If picket stake is used, cut a good, solid one the horse can't break. Drive it in deep and solid so it won't be pulled out.

Sometimes picketing by a foot is preferred to tying by halter. Horses sometimes get a shod hind foot caught in a halter when scratching head with hind foot.

All horses must be trained to picket, but once they learn what it's all about, picketing by foot is safest.

One hobble strap and a swivel on 30' of rope works just fine.

TRAINING THE PACK HORSE

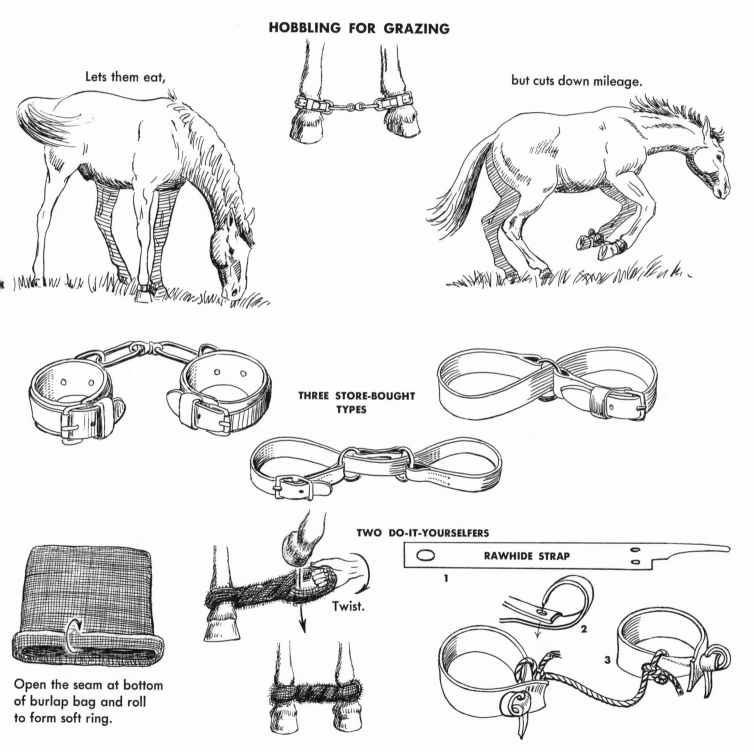

HOBBLING FOR GRAZING

Lets them eat,

but cuts down mileage.

THREE STORE-BOUGHT TYPES

TWO DO-IT-YOURSELFERS

Open the seam at bottom of burlap bag and roll to form soft ring.

Twist.

RAWHIDE STRAP

1

2

3

TRAINING THE PACK HORSE

Get your pack horse used to all the strange things he will have to carry, from stoves to bear hides.

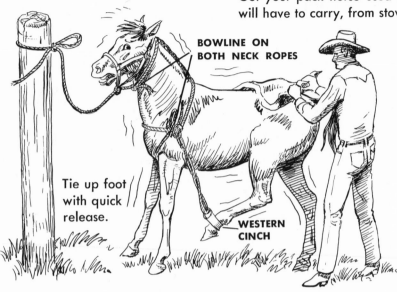

BOWLINE ON BOTH NECK ROPES

Tie up foot with quick release.

WESTERN CINCH

Sack him down (rub or touch him) with any frightening piece of equipment that might touch him off on the trail.

BEAR HID[E]

If you intend to bring in big game like bear, a horse should be introduced to i[t] ahead of time.

Of course there is always the old food trick. If there's one thing a horse isn't afraid of it's the smell of food—associate that with the gear and he just may tolerate it.

Then too a pack horse ought to be trained not to spook at the least little noise.

CRASH-BANG !!

PROOF-TESTED INDIFFERENCE

TRAINING THE PACK HORSE

TAILING-UP

Make sure your pack horses are well acquainted with this type of hitch and each other before heading for the hills. If there isn't good co-operation among the horses your cargo may get the worst of it.

SOME GOOD TAIL HITCHES

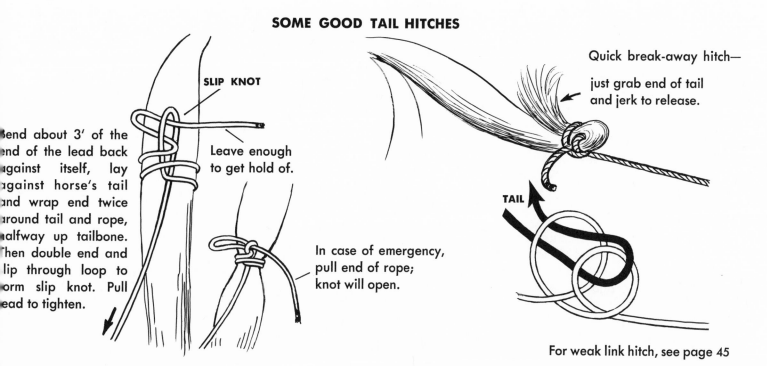

SLIP KNOT

Leave enough to get hold of.

Send about 3' of the end of the lead back against itself, lay against horse's tail and wrap end twice around tail and rope, halfway up tailbone. Then double end and slip through loop to form slip knot. Pull lead to tighten.

In case of emergency, pull end of rope; knot will open.

Quick break-away hitch—

just grab end of tail and jerk to release.

TAIL

For weak link hitch, see page 45

REPLACING A SHOE

All wilderness riders should know how to tighten or replace a loose shoe. A farrier can teach you in a few minutes how to do it.

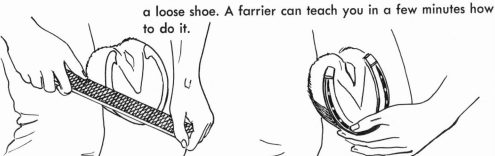

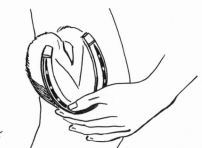

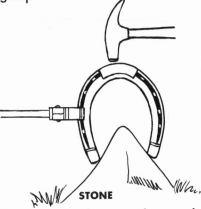

Stand touching horse with your side while facing to the rear of horse. Run your hand down leg to grasp fetlock.

Lift foot and hold between knees, clean sole and frog. Smooth surface to receive shoe. Work in close; horse will be more comfortable, less apt to pull away.

If old shoe is to be replaced—no problem. If new shoe, check the fit.

Checkered face this side so beveled point will turn out.

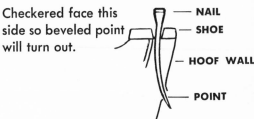

— NAIL
— SHOE
— HOOF WALL
— POINT

Too narrow—heat and pound with ends over stone to open the shoe to fit.

STONE

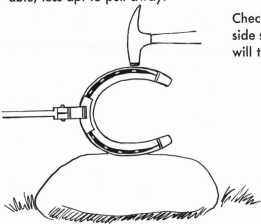

Too wide—heat and pound ends together to fit.

When nail head is driven in as far as it will go, grab the point at once with claws of hammer and twist off. If you fail to do so and the horse pulls his foot away, you could have the nail point in your leg.

— HAMMER
— SHOE

HOOF WALL

Smooth any cracks from nails with rasp.

Then hold rasp under twisted-off nail and hit head to clinch against hoof wall.

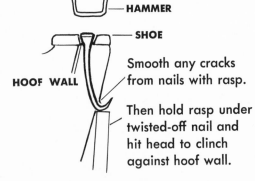

Complete the clinch with the hammer.

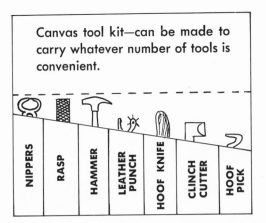

Canvas tool kit—can be made to carry whatever number of tools is convenient.

NIPPERS | RASP | HAMMER | LEATHER PUNCH | HOOF KNIFE | CLINCH CUTTER | HOOF PICK

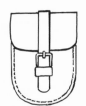

A couple of horse shoes carried in small saddle pockets can solve the problem of a lost shoe.

ROPES-TOOLS OF THE PACKER'S TRADE

YOU MUST MAKE UP YOUR OWN TO SUIT YOUR NEEDS

To prevent end of rope from unwinding, use whipping or crown splice.

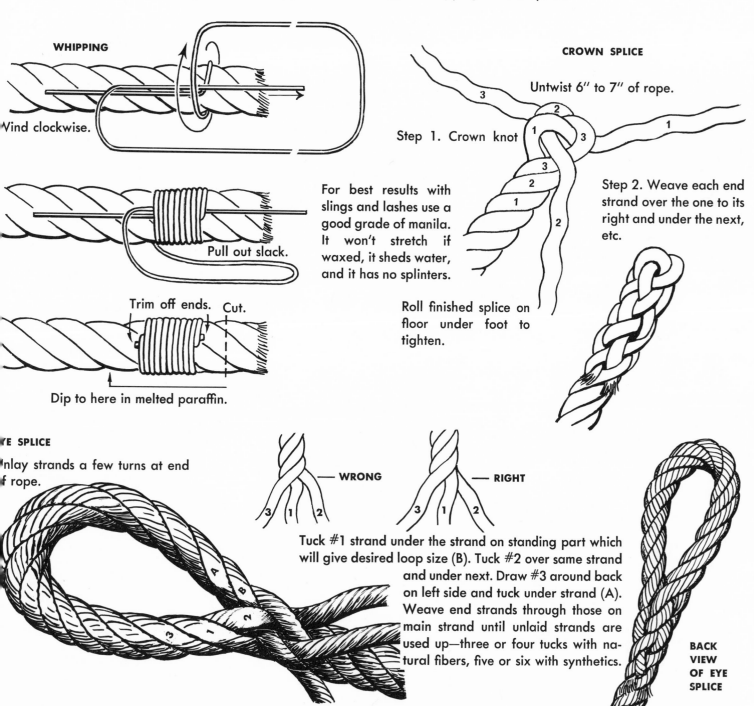

WHIPPING

Wind clockwise.

Pull out slack.

Trim off ends. Cut.

Dip to here in melted paraffin.

CROWN SPLICE

Untwist 6" to 7" of rope.

Step 1. Crown knot

For best results with slings and lashes use a good grade of manila. It won't stretch if waxed, it sheds water, and it has no splinters.

Step 2. Weave each end strand over the one to its right and under the next, etc.

Roll finished splice on floor under foot to tighten.

EYE SPLICE

Unlay strands a few turns at end of rope.

— WRONG

— RIGHT

Tuck #1 strand under the strand on standing part which will give desired loop size (B). Tuck #2 over same strand and under next. Draw #3 around back on left side and tuck under strand (A). Weave end strands through those on main strand until unlaid strands are used up—three or four tucks with natural fibers, five or six with synthetics.

BACK VIEW OF EYE SPLICE

ROPES-TOOLS OF THE PACKER'S TRADE

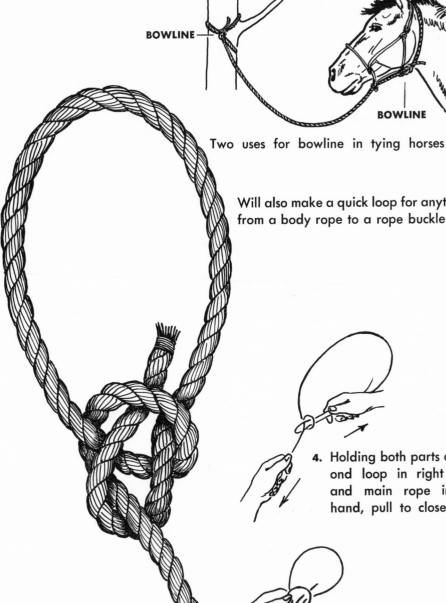

THE BOWLINE

Probably the best way to remember it is to think that it's one loop passed through another to catch hold of the main rope.

BOWLINE

BOWLINE

Two uses for bowline in tying horses

Will also make a quick loop for anything from a body rope to a rope buckle.

1. Rotate rope one-half turn to the right with right thumb and forefinger to form first loop.

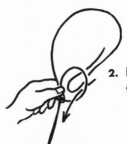

2. Pass second loop through first loop.

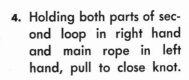

4. Holding both parts of second loop in right hand and main rope in left hand, pull to close knot.

3. Bring end of rope through the loop and around the main rope and back through first loop.

ROPES-TOOLS OF THE PACKER'S TRADE

OVERHAND HONDA KNOT

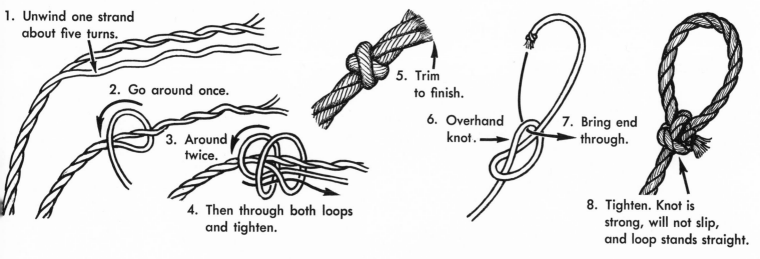

1. Unwind one strand about five turns.

2. Go around once.

3. Around twice.

4. Then through both loops and tighten.

5. Trim to finish.

6. Overhand knot.

7. Bring end through.

8. Tighten. Knot is strong, will not slip, and loop stands straight.

ROPE HALTERS

Rotate loop one complete turn so when lead is pulled pressure is transferred to neck loop and doesn't just tighten up on nose loop.

When lead end is pulled, one-half turn will tighten nose loop.

ONE COMPLETE TURN

EASY LARIAT LOOP TYPE HALTER

Make nose loop by passing rope end through lariat loop.

Hold both sections of rope at A with left hand to maintain nose loop. Hold B with right hand and slip onto head.

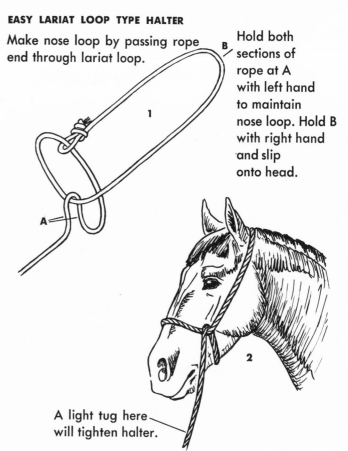

A light tug here will tighten halter.

ROPES-TOOLS OF THE PACKER'S TRADE

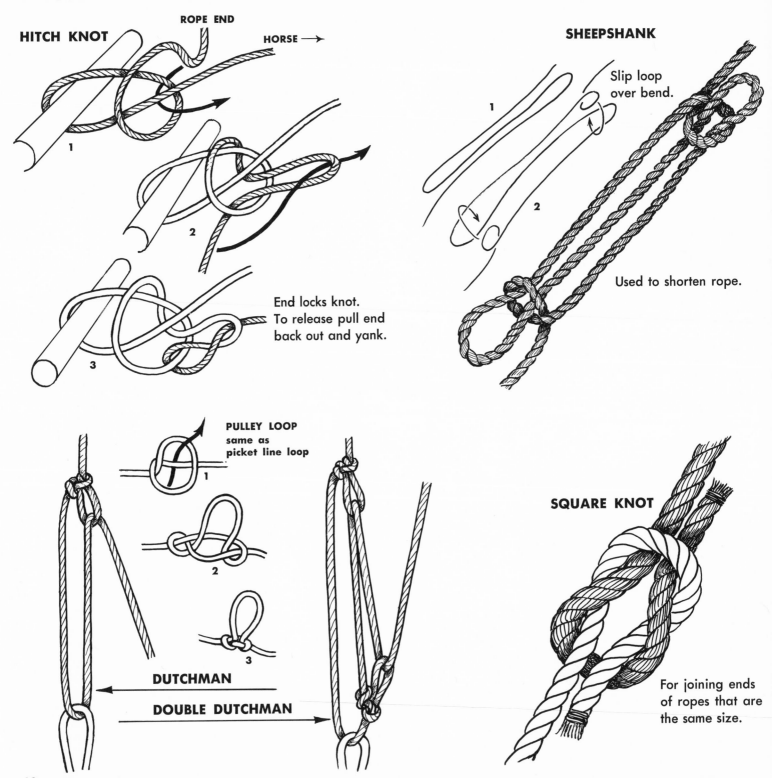

HITCH KNOT

ROPE END

HORSE →

1

2

3

End locks knot.
To release pull end
back out and yank.

SHEEPSHANK

1

Slip loop
over bend.

2

Used to shorten rope.

PULLEY LOOP
same as
picket line loop

1

2

3

DUTCHMAN

DOUBLE DUTCHMAN

SQUARE KNOT

For joining ends
of ropes that are
the same size.

BASIC ROPE WORK AND KNOT TYING

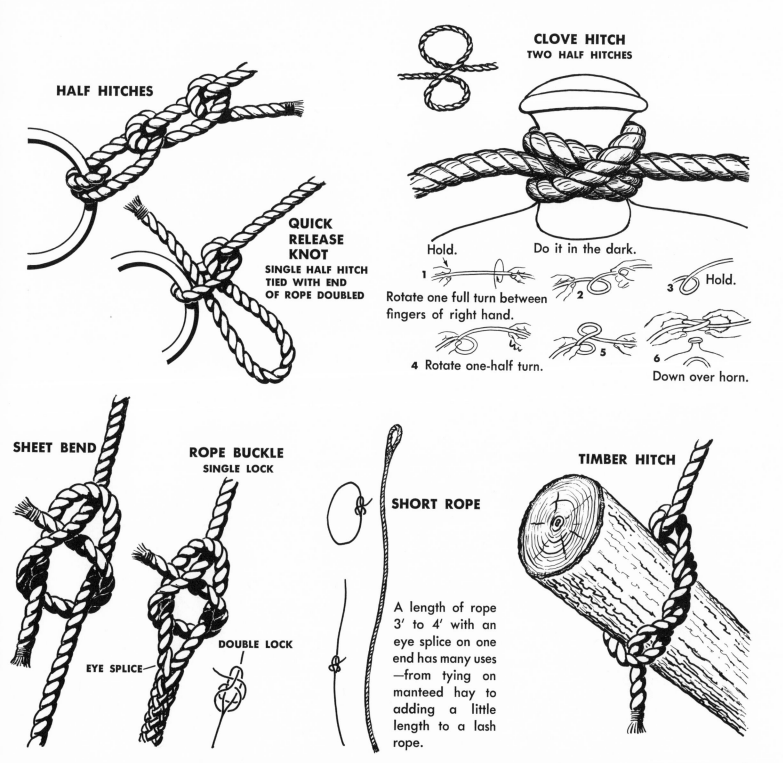

HALF HITCHES

QUICK RELEASE KNOT
SINGLE HALF HITCH TIED WITH END OF ROPE DOUBLED

CLOVE HITCH
TWO HALF HITCHES

Hold.

Do it in the dark.

1 Rotate one full turn between fingers of right hand.

2

3 Hold.

4 Rotate one-half turn.

5

6

Down over horn.

SHEET BEND

ROPE BUCKLE
SINGLE LOCK

EYE SPLICE

DOUBLE LOCK

SHORT ROPE

A length of rope 3' to 4' with an eye splice on one end has many uses —from tying on manteed hay to adding a little length to a lash rope.

TIMBER HITCH

QUICK-TIE–QUICK-RELEASE TIES

SLIDING CLOVE HITCH TO MANTEE HAY OR GRAIN, ETC.

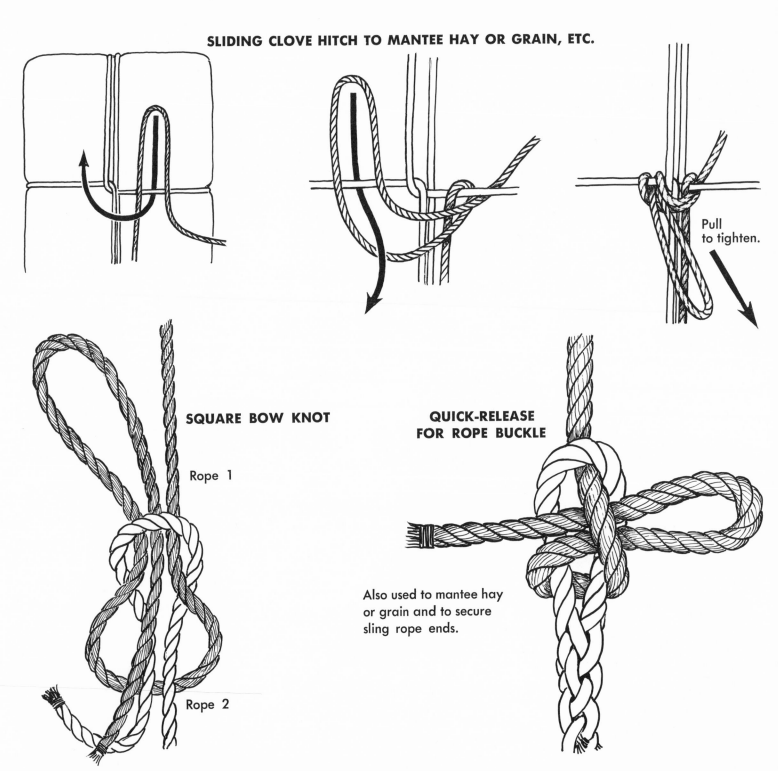

Pull to tighten.

SQUARE BOW KNOT

Rope 1

Rope 2

QUICK-RELEASE FOR ROPE BUCKLE

Also used to mantee hay or grain and to secure sling rope ends.

NECESSARY ITEMS FOR HORSE PACKING

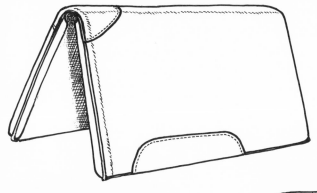

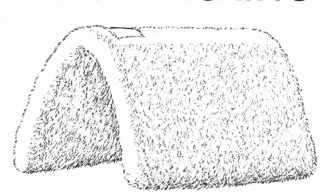

SPECIAL PACK SADDLE PADS

LEATHER-REINFORCED 33″ x 34″ HEAVY ARMY DUCK COVER— 2″ POLY FOAM PAD

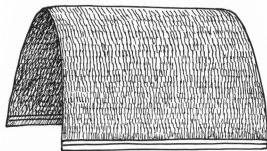

30″ x 36″ "COOLBACK" PACK SADDLE PAD— a washable fleecelike material which prevents galls and sores

Covers made of the same material for breast collar, breeching, halter, and cinch end (shown below) are also available.

If you don't have a special pack saddle pad, use a washable hair blanket under a thick, quilted pad.

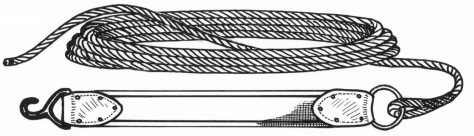

CINCH END COVER

LASH ROPE—45′ OF GOOD ½″ MANILA ROPE (waxed, no splinters) eye spliced to **LASH CINCH**—extra heavy cotton duck webbing with ring and hook ends reinforced with leather

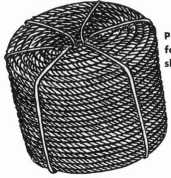

PLENTY OF EXTRA ROPE for picketing, camp use, short ropes, etc.

TARPS 6′ x 8′, 8′ x 10′, or about that size will do just fine.

CANVAS PACK COVER

Most any tarp that would be used around camp can be folded and lashed over the pack to keep it together and dry.

HORSE LUGGAGE

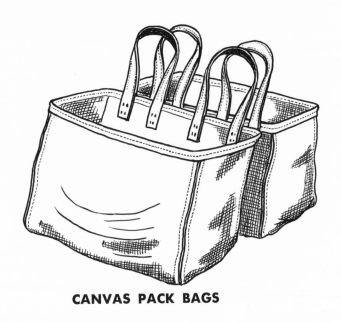

CANVAS PACK BAGS

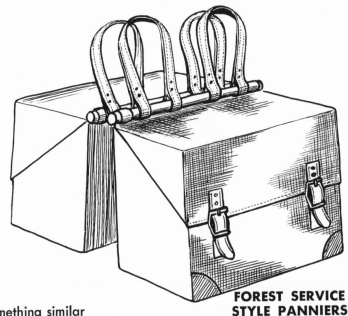

**FOREST SERVICE
STYLE PANNIERS**

Panniers shown above or something similar
may be purchased from saddle shops.

Below are two homemade types. You may wish
to design a set tailored to your particular needs.

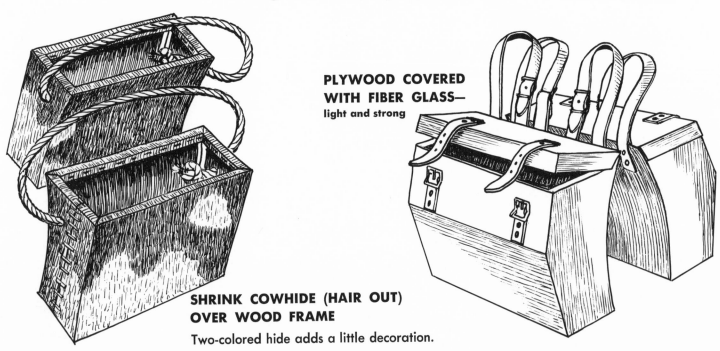

**PLYWOOD COVERED
WITH FIBER GLASS—**
light and strong

**SHRINK COWHIDE (HAIR OUT)
OVER WOOD FRAME**

Two-colored hide adds a little decoration.

HUMANE HORSE PACK SADDLE

"Humane" is the name of this particular model, which differs from the "standard" sawbuck by having bars that fit better to the horse's back.

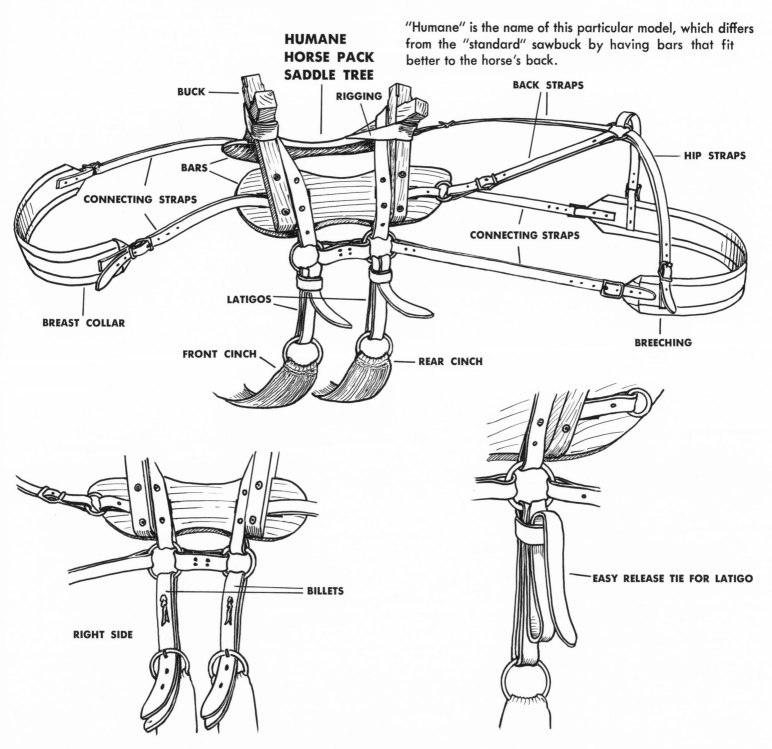

HUMANE HORSE PACK SADDLE TREE

BUCK

RIGGING

BACK STRAPS

HIP STRAPS

BARS

CONNECTING STRAPS

CONNECTING STRAPS

BREAST COLLAR

LATIGOS

BREECHING

FRONT CINCH

REAR CINCH

BILLETS

RIGHT SIDE

EASY RELEASE TIE FOR LATIGO

DECKER PACK SADDLE

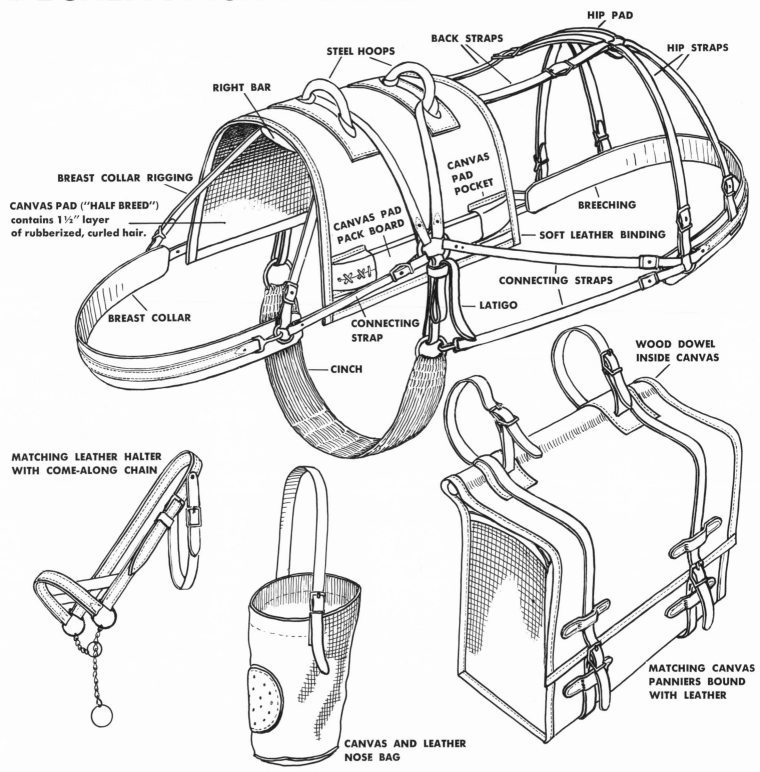

STEEL HOOPS

BACK STRAPS

HIP PAD

HIP STRAPS

RIGHT BAR

BREAST COLLAR RIGGING

CANVAS PAD ("HALF BREED") contains 1½" layer of rubberized, curled hair.

CANVAS PAD POCKET

CANVAS PAD PACK BOARD

BREECHING

SOFT LEATHER BINDING

CONNECTING STRAPS

BREAST COLLAR

LATIGO

CONNECTING STRAP

CINCH

WOOD DOWEL INSIDE CANVAS

MATCHING LEATHER HALTER WITH COME-ALONG CHAIN

CANVAS AND LEATHER NOSE BAG

MATCHING CANVAS PANNIERS BOUND WITH LEATHER

CANVAS SADDLE PANNIERS

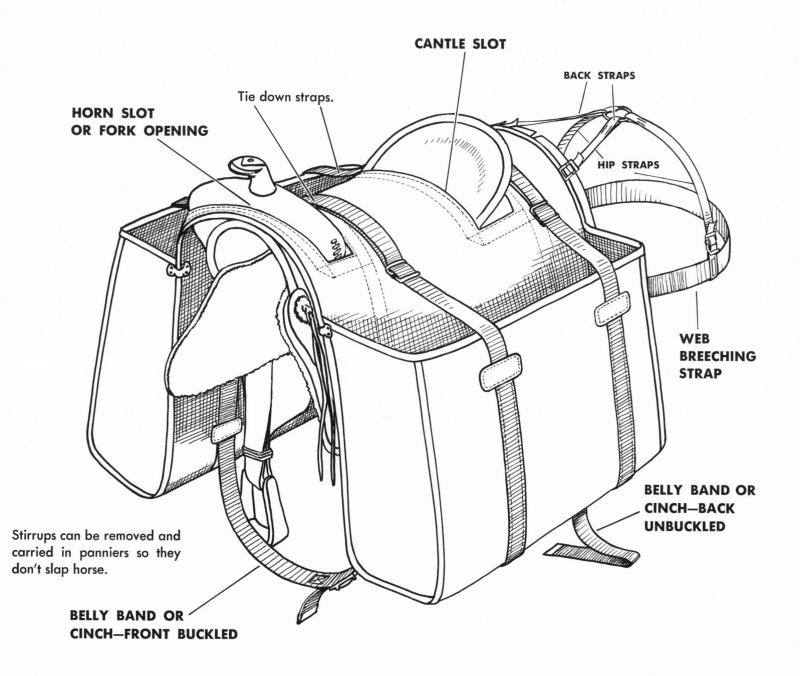

CANTLE SLOT

BACK STRAPS

Tie down straps.

HORN SLOT
OR FORK OPENING

HIP STRAPS

WEB
BREECHING
STRAP

BELLY BAND OR
CINCH—BACK
UNBUCKLED

Stirrups can be removed and
carried in panniers so they
don't slap horse.

BELLY BAND OR
CINCH—FRONT BUCKLED

SLINGS FOR SECURING CARGO

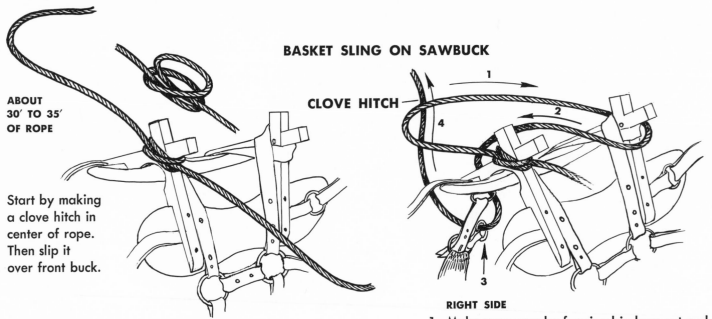

ABOUT 30' TO 35' OF ROPE

Start by making a clove hitch in center of rope. Then slip it over front buck.

BASKET SLING ON SAWBUCK

CLOVE HITCH

RIGHT SIDE

1. Make cross rope by forming big loop out and around back buck.

2. Run end of rope down through sling ring #3 and up outside cross rope as shown in #4.

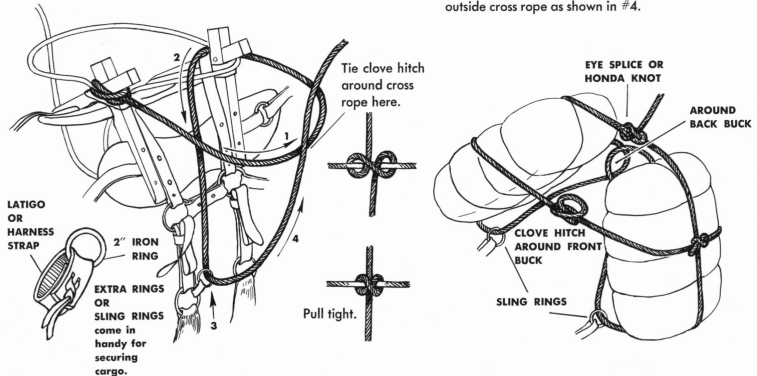

Tie clove hitch around cross rope here.

Pull tight.

LATIGO OR HARNESS STRAP

2" IRON RING

EXTRA RINGS OR SLING RINGS come in handy for securing cargo.

EYE SPLICE OR HONDA KNOT

AROUND BACK BUCK

CLOVE HITCH AROUND FRONT BUCK

SLING RINGS

SLINGS FOR SECURING CARGO

BARREL SLING ON SAWBUCK

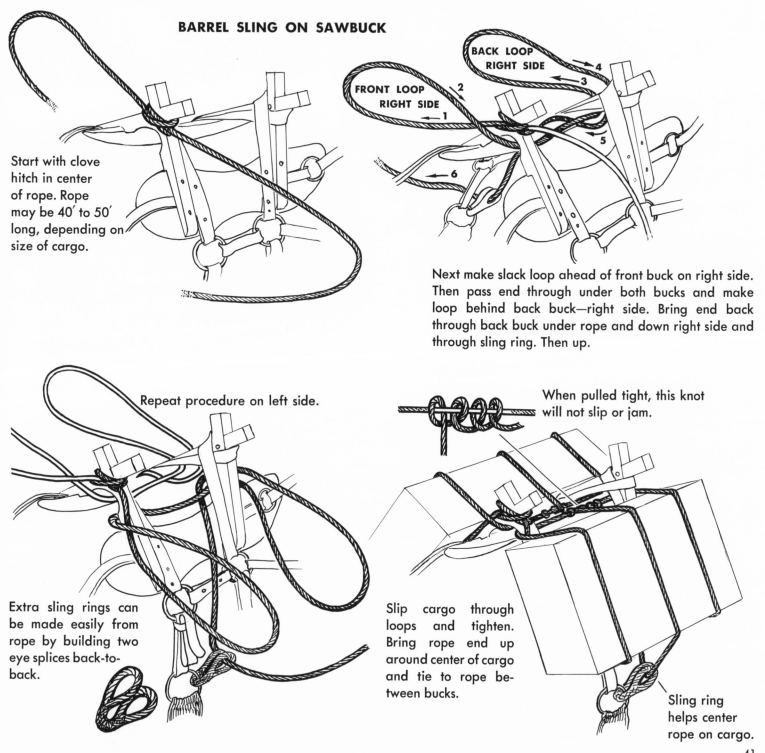

Start with clove hitch in center of rope. Rope may be 40' to 50' long, depending on size of cargo.

FRONT LOOP RIGHT SIDE
←1 2

BACK LOOP RIGHT SIDE
→4 3
←5
←6

Next make slack loop ahead of front buck on right side. Then pass end through under both bucks and make loop behind back buck—right side. Bring end back through back buck under rope and down right side and through sling ring. Then up.

Repeat procedure on left side.

Extra sling rings can be made easily from rope by building two eye splices back-to-back.

When pulled tight, this knot will not slip or jam.

Slip cargo through loops and tighten. Bring rope end up around center of cargo and tie to rope between bucks.

Sling ring helps center rope on cargo.

SLINGS FOR SECURING CARGO

SAWBUCK

FRONT BUCK OR HOOP

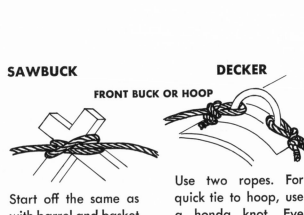

Start off the same as with barrel and basket slings.

DECKER

Use two ropes. For quick tie to hoop, use a honda knot. Eye splice or bowline can be used also.

CROWFOOT SLING

Fast to saddle's front hoop, rope is drawn around the front of cargo to saddle's back hoop, then down the back, under, and up the center on front side of cargo.

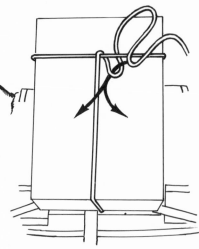

One loop is brought down behind horizontal portion. Another loop is then passed through it. The first is pulled tight. The second is spread to go over bottom of cargo.

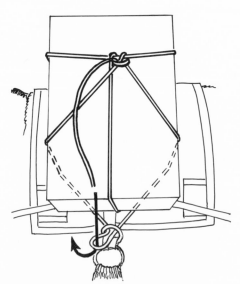

Allow enough slack so loop made at the bottom can slip through sling ring on cinch. End of rope is then threaded through small loop . . .

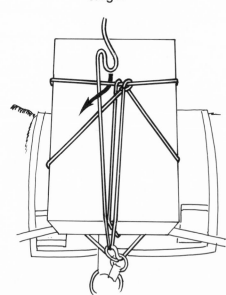

. . . and pulled up to horizontal portion of rope. There another loop is shoved down behind the horizontal and brought forward.

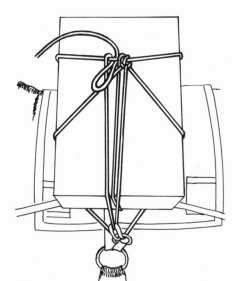

This loop is secured with two half hitches from end of rope as shown here.

42

SLINGS FOR SECURING CARGO

ADAPTATIONS TO THE DECKER

To fasten ends of the rope on top, use eye splice, honda knot, or bowline loop. Tie off with rope buckle or half hitches.

All knots shown are clove hitches.

BASKET SLING

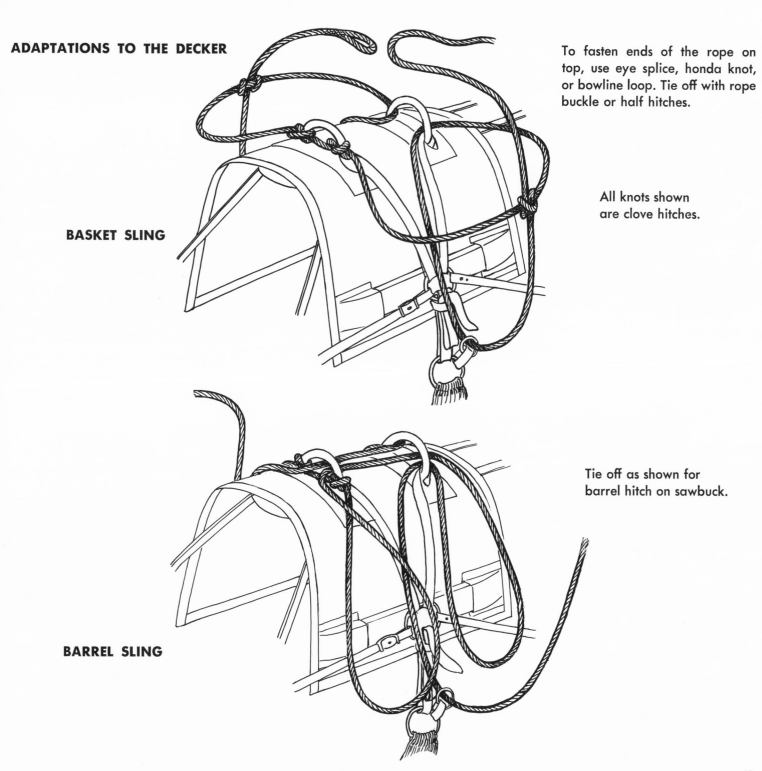

Tie off as shown for barrel hitch on sawbuck.

BARREL SLING

MAKING TANDEM HITCHES AND TIES

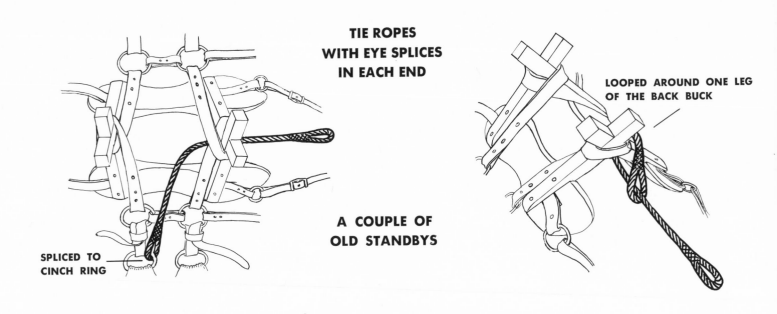

TIE ROPES WITH EYE SPLICES IN EACH END

LOOPED AROUND ONE LEG OF THE BACK BUCK

A COUPLE OF OLD STANDBYS

SPLICED TO CINCH RING

NEW TWO-ROPE HITCH

To tie nylon, poly, etc. to cinch ring, seal end of rope by burning. Then use clincher knot.

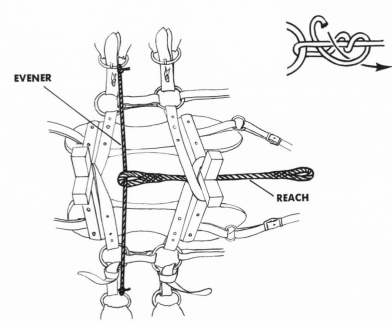

EVENER

REACH

Evener is made of ¼" or ⅜" nylon; it makes no big lump under cinch ring to dig into horse's side.

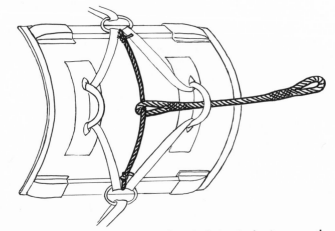

On the decker, evener can be tied to cinch rings or the rings in the rigging. This kind of hitch distributes any angle of pull from the rear to both sides of the rig and prevents shifting.

MAKING TANDEM HITCHES AND TIES

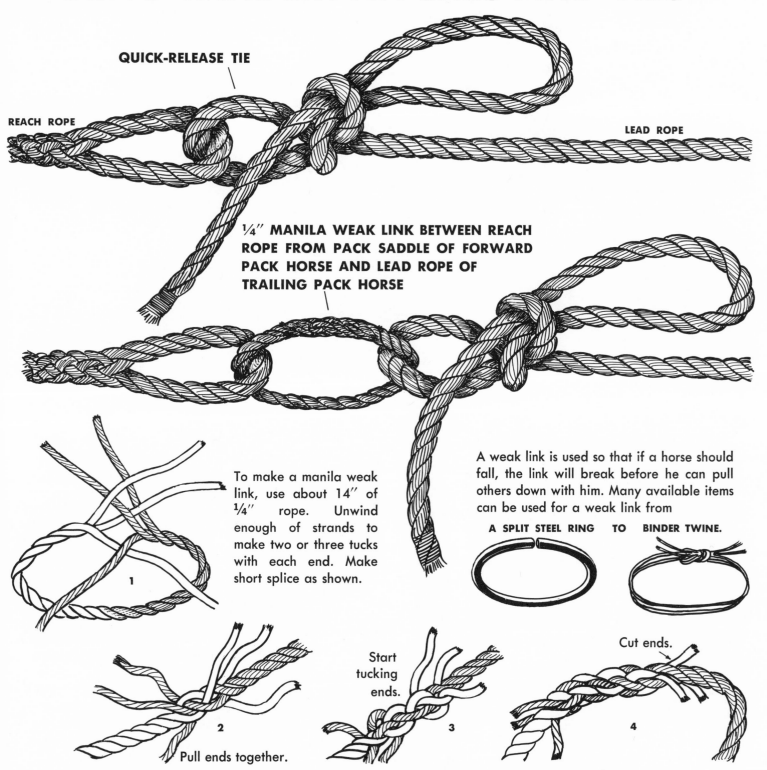

QUICK-RELEASE TIE

REACH ROPE

LEAD ROPE

¼″ **MANILA WEAK LINK BETWEEN REACH ROPE FROM PACK SADDLE OF FORWARD PACK HORSE AND LEAD ROPE OF TRAILING PACK HORSE**

To make a manila weak link, use about 14″ of ¼″ rope. Unwind enough of strands to make two or three tucks with each end. Make short splice as shown.

1

A weak link is used so that if a horse should fall, the link will break before he can pull others down with him. Many available items can be used for a weak link from

A SPLIT STEEL RING   TO   BINDER TWINE.

Pull ends together.

2

Start tucking ends.

3

Cut ends.

4

PREPARING FEED FOR SLINGING

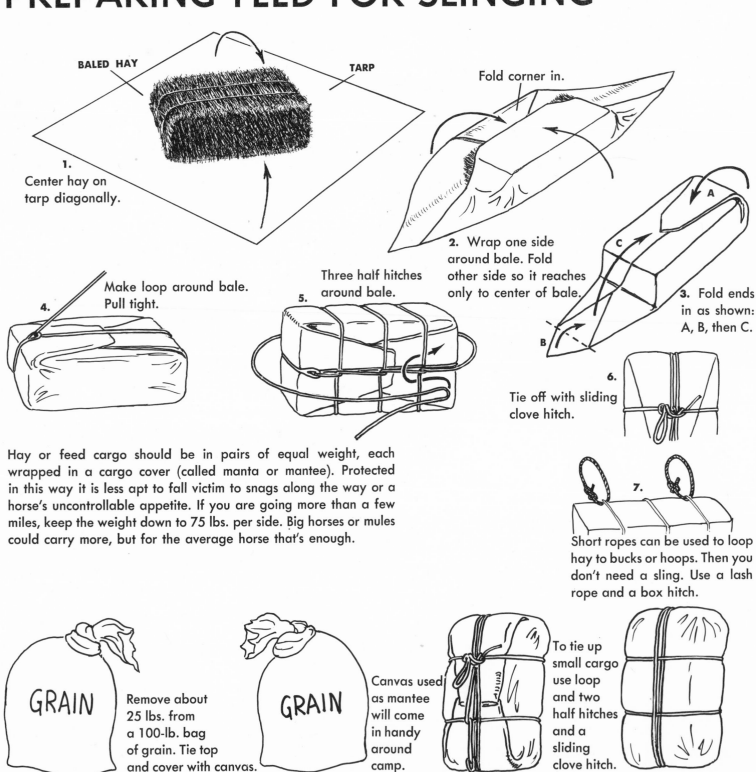

BALED HAY

TARP

1. Center hay on tarp diagonally.

Fold corner in.

2. Wrap one side around bale. Fold other side so it reaches only to center of bale.

3. Fold ends in as shown: A, B, then C.

4. Make loop around bale. Pull tight.

Three half hitches around bale.

5.

6. Tie off with sliding clove hitch.

7.

Hay or feed cargo should be in pairs of equal weight, each wrapped in a cargo cover (called manta or mantee). Protected in this way it is less apt to fall victim to snags along the way or a horse's uncontrollable appetite. If you are going more than a few miles, keep the weight down to 75 lbs. per side. Big horses or mules could carry more, but for the average horse that's enough.

Short ropes can be used to loop hay to bucks or hoops. Then you don't need a sling. Use a lash rope and a box hitch.

GRAIN

Remove about 25 lbs. from a 100-lb. bag of grain. Tie top and cover with canvas.

GRAIN

Canvas used as mantee will come in handy around camp.

To tie up small cargo use loop and two half hitches and a sliding clove hitch.

PACKING OUT YOUR GAME

Two front quarters of a deer manteed and ready for a long trip out. Right quarter on left side and left on right, inside out.

Here hindquarters are manteed and slung upside down and inside out.

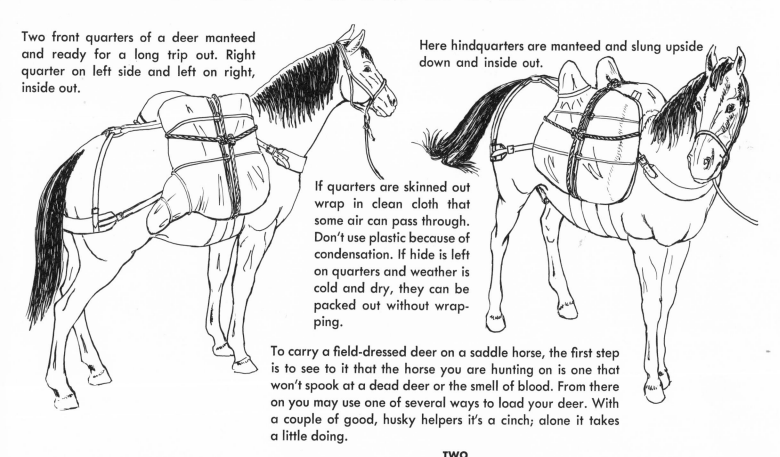

If quarters are skinned out wrap in clean cloth that some air can pass through. Don't use plastic because of condensation. If hide is left on quarters and weather is cold and dry, they can be packed out without wrapping.

To carry a field-dressed deer on a saddle horse, the first step is to see to it that the horse you are hunting on is one that won't spook at a dead deer or the smell of blood. From there on you may use one of several ways to load your deer. With a couple of good, husky helpers it's a cinch; alone it takes a little doing.

However you get your buck aboard your four-footed friend, whether you climb up on top and pull him up by the antlers or slide the rear end over the saddle from the left side, the deer should lie over the saddle with his front end on the left side and rear end on the right. A dead deer is a slippery character and will slide off at the first chance. To keep him in place, before loading cut a slit (just large enough to slip over the saddle horn) in the skin a couple of inches to the right of the place where the last ribs from both sides meet. When this is hooked

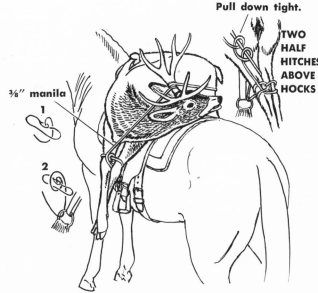

TWO HALF HITCHES Pull down tight.

TWO HALF HITCHES ABOVE HOCKS

⅜" manila
1
2

over the horn and the head is pulled back with horns up, the deer should be pretty well balanced. The buck's front legs should be tied to the left cinch ring, the hind legs to the right. Head should be tied securely so it won't flop and so antlers can't jab the horse. If you cut off the buck's legs, cut below the knee and hock joints so you can make tie slits that will hold under the tendons above the joints. Saddle strings if long enough can be used to tie on a deer, but play it safe and take enough rope along to do the job right.

LASH ELK ANTLERS ON SECURELY

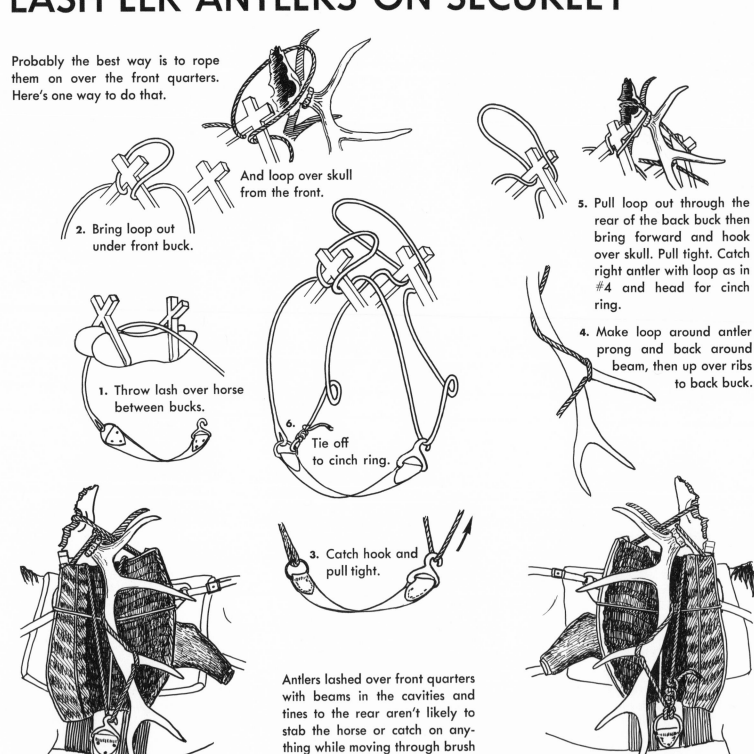

Probably the best way is to rope them on over the front quarters. Here's one way to do that.

And loop over skull from the front.

2. Bring loop out under front buck.

1. Throw lash over horse between bucks.

6. Tie off to cinch ring.

3. Catch hook and pull tight.

5. Pull loop out through the rear of the back buck then bring forward and hook over skull. Pull tight. Catch right antler with loop as in #4 and head for cinch ring.

4. Make loop around antler prong and back around beam, then up over ribs to back buck.

Antlers lashed over front quarters with beams in the cavities and tines to the rear aren't likely to stab the horse or catch on anything while moving through brush or trees.

LEFT SIDE

RIGHT SIDE

DECIDING ON THE RIGHT HITCH

SOFT PANNIERS (CANVAS PACK BAGS) WITH LARGE TARP OR TENT FOLDED AND PLACED ACROSS TOP

SIMILAR LOAD WITH BEDROLLS

SQUAW HITCH shown here can be used to secure many kinds of loads.

HORSE HEADING ←

SQUAW HITCH—ONE OF THE EASIEST AND QUICKEST TO LEARN AND USE

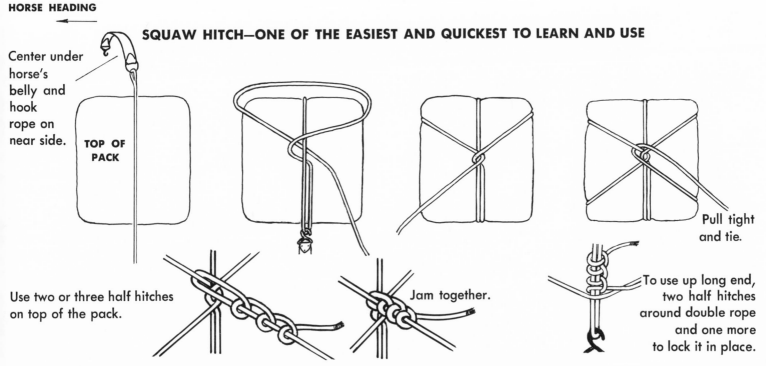

Center under horse's belly and hook rope on near side.

TOP OF PACK

Pull tight and tie.

Use two or three half hitches on top of the pack.

Jam together.

To use up long end, two half hitches around double rope and one more to lock it in place.

DECIDING ON THE RIGHT HITCH

The "ring" hitch is similar to the squaw hitch.

THE O.A. "RING" HITCH

Similar to the squaw hitch but uses ring.

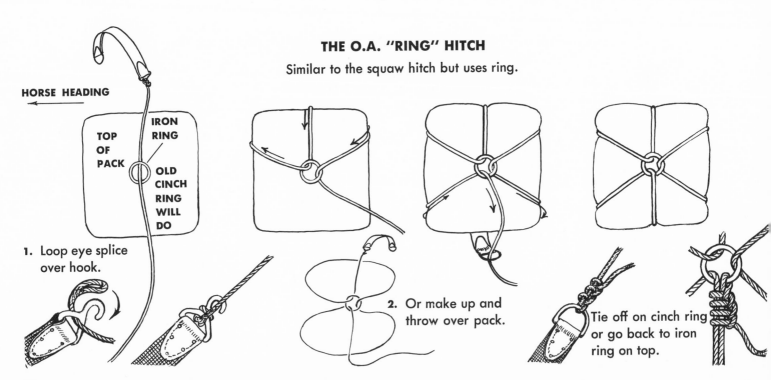

HORSE HEADING

TOP OF PACK

IRON RING

OLD CINCH RING WILL DO

1. Loop eye splice over hook.

2. Or make up and throw over pack.

Tie off on cinch ring or go back to iron ring on top.

DECIDING ON THE RIGHT HITCH

WOODEN PANNIERS AND SLEEPING BAGS

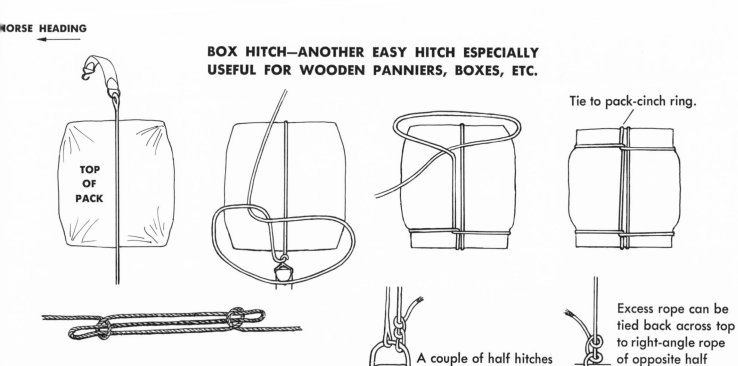

HORSE HEADING ←

BOX HITCH—ANOTHER EASY HITCH ESPECIALLY USEFUL FOR WOODEN PANNIERS, BOXES, ETC.

TOP
OF
PACK

Tie to pack-cinch ring.

To shorten end of rope use a sheepshank not a knife.

A couple of half hitches to tie to lash-cinch ring.

Excess rope can be tied back across top to right-angle rope of opposite half hitch.

DECIDING ON THE RIGHT HITCH

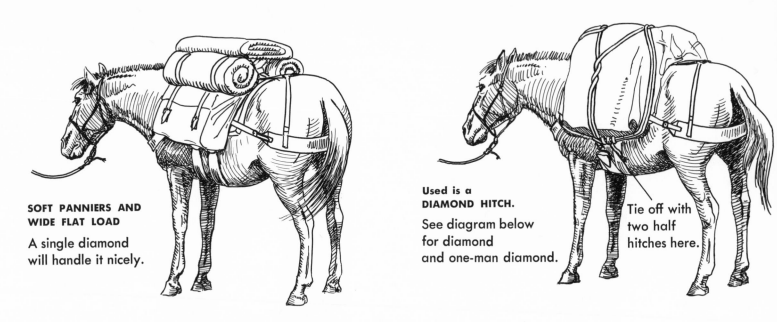

SOFT PANNIERS AND WIDE FLAT LOAD

A single diamond will handle it nicely.

Used is a **DIAMOND HITCH.**

See diagram below for diamond and one-man diamond.

Tie off with two half hitches here.

Diamonds are a packer's best friend or they'll do till one comes along.

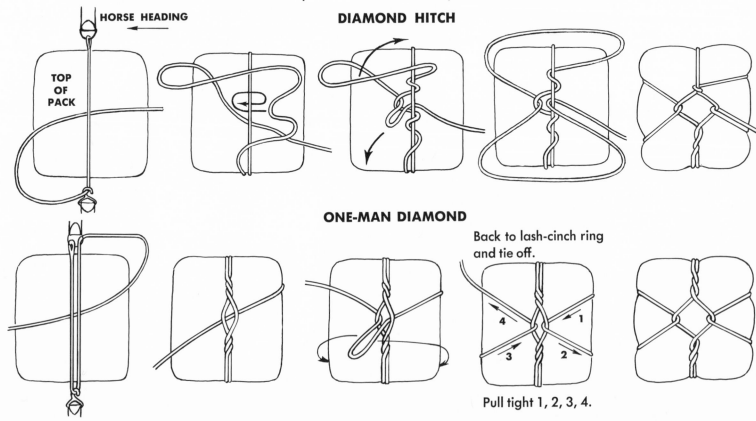

HORSE HEADING ←

TOP OF PACK

DIAMOND HITCH

ONE-MAN DIAMOND

Back to lash-cinch ring and tie off.

4 1
3 2

Pull tight 1, 2, 3, 4.

DECIDING ON THE RIGHT HITCH

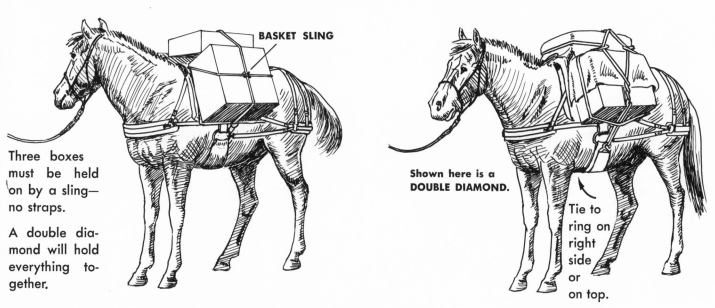

BASKET SLING

Three boxes must be held on by a sling—no straps.

A double diamond will hold everything together.

Shown here is a **DOUBLE DIAMOND.**

Tie to ring on right side or on top.

A double diamond can be made to fit and hold odd-shaped cargo.

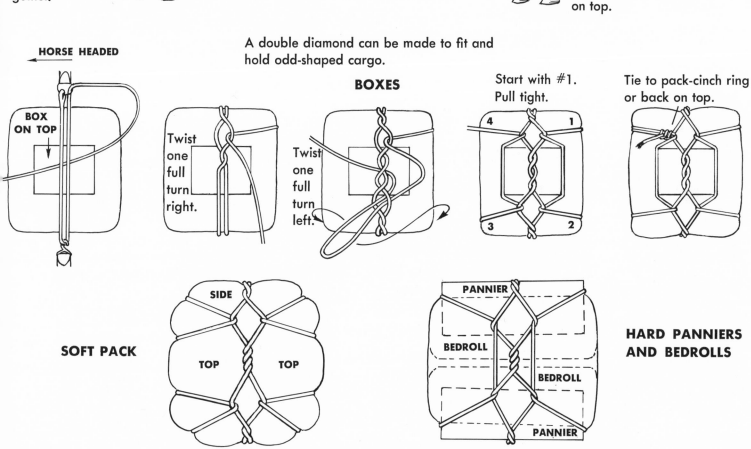

← **HORSE HEADED**

BOX ON TOP

BOXES

Twist one full turn right.

Twist one full turn left.

Start with #1. Pull tight.

4   1

3   2

Tie to pack-cinch ring or back on top.

SIDE

TOP   **TOP**

SOFT PACK

PANNIER

BEDROLL

BEDROLL

PANNIER

HARD PANNIERS AND BEDROLLS

WHAT TO TAKE AND HOW MUCH

Carefully calculate each meal of each day. Weigh time and needs as accurately as possible for yourself and your animals, and try to bite off only what you can chew. After all, this is supposed to be a fun trip.

WHAT TO TAKE AND HOW MUCH

MEALS FOR TWO RIDERS FOR WEEKEND FISHING PACK TRIP			
	BREAKFAST	**LUNCH**	**SUPPER**
Friday		*TRAIL LUNCH* Cheese sandwiches Instant drink mix & H₂O Fruit bars	Steak Eggs Instant potatoes Peas Biscuits Peaches Coffee
Saturday	Tang Instant oatmeal Biscuits Canadian bacon Eggs Coffee	*FISHING LUNCH* 6 Peanut butter and jelly sandwiches 2 Cup-a-Soup Candy Dry fruit Dry milk	Chunky soup over instant rice Trout if any Biscuits Coffee
Sunday	Pancakes Eggs Bacon Coffee	*TRAIL LUNCH* Jerky Fruit cake Instant drink	

When you and another rider go on a pack trip, your four-legged packing buddy must carry the needs of five—two riders and three horses. Now let's say his load is limited to about 150 lbs. The determining factor in how long you can stay is whether you're heading for belly-high grass or just a pile of rocks. The more food your horse must haul for himself and the other horses, the less he can haul for you.

Plan your meals in advance. Take only what you need.

First aid kits, tools, and a small scale go in saddle bags, fishing gear in cantle pack. (If your fishing rod is in two pieces it can go on the pack horse if the pieces are in a plastic pipe with rubber ends taped on.) Your ax goes in a rifle scabbard on the riding saddle. Put bags of soft goods between and in noisy pots to quiet them. Hard panniers or heavy canvas ones work very well for this kind of trip.

Light sleeping bags and tarp for shelter (or very light tent—make do where you can) can go behind saddles.

Fill kettles and coffee pot—use all possible space.

PLAN FOOD RATIONS IN ADVANCE

MAKE A LIST AND FOLLOW IT AS CLOSELY AS POSSIBLE.

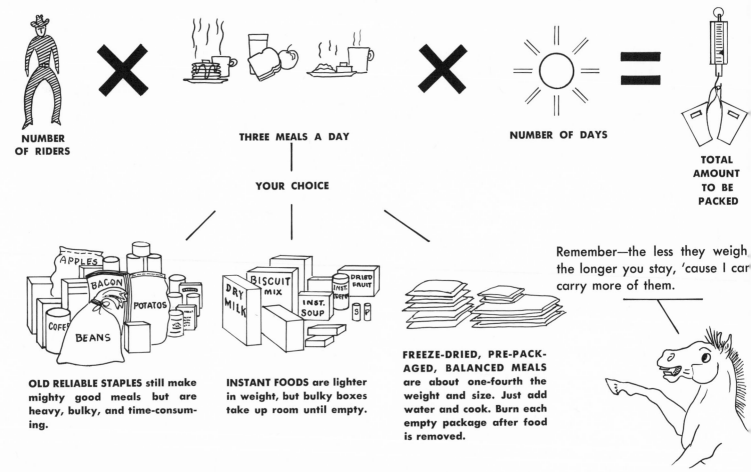

NUMBER OF RIDERS × **THREE MEALS A DAY** × **NUMBER OF DAYS** = **TOTAL AMOUNT TO BE PACKED**

YOUR CHOICE

OLD RELIABLE STAPLES still make mighty good meals but are heavy, bulky, and time-consuming.

INSTANT FOODS are lighter in weight, but bulky boxes take up room until empty.

FREEZE-DRIED, PRE-PACKAGED, BALANCED MEALS are about one-fourth the weight and size. Just add water and cook. Burn each empty package after food is removed.

Remember—the less they weigh, the longer you stay, 'cause I can carry more of them.

TO PREVENT MONOTONY IF YOUR TRIP LASTS A WEEK OR MORE

Strive for at least three variations of each meal.

	BREAKFAST	LUNCH	DINNER
1			
2			
3			

Chances are that before you finish planning the meals for your trip you will have used items from all three of the above groups and the menus will have been determined by your preferences, so no menus are offered here. However, this method of selecting amounts of necessary foods should prevent running out ahead of time. Of course on hunting and fishing trips the game can add a tasty supplement to your regular food supply.

LOADING THE PANNIERS

PRACTICE ESTIMATING WEIGHT AND LOADING IN CASE SCALES ARE LOST, FORGOTTEN, OR BROKEN.

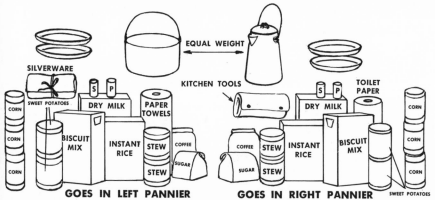

EQUAL WEIGHT

SILVERWARE

KITCHEN TOOLS

TOILET PAPER

GOES IN LEFT PANNIER

GOES IN RIGHT PANNIER

Put half the cans or boxes of each item in each pannier.

3-lb. coffee can makes a good measure for feeding horses. Use the same can to load feed in panniers, putting the same number of canfuls in each.

COFFEE CAN

When feeding take from one pannier and then the other to keep the load even.

WEIGHT PAINTED OR STAMPED ON ITEMS HELPS PACKER TO KEEP LOAD EVEN.

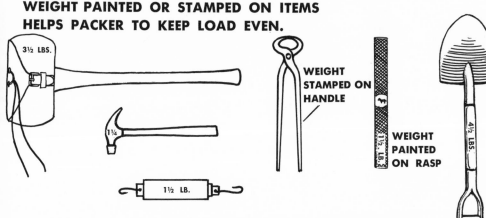

3½ LBS.

1¼

1½ LB.

WEIGHT STAMPED ON HANDLE

WEIGHT PAINTED ON RASP

1½ LB.

4½ LBS.

ODDS AND ENDS TUBE, FISHING ROD CASE, ETC.
Paint weight on side.

ODDS & ENDS 2 LBS.

BULL BELL 1 LB.

GAS CAMP STOVE   15 LBS.

HOW TO HANDLE RAW EGGS

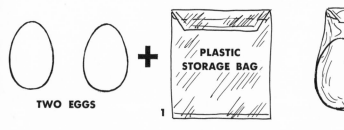

TWO EGGS

+

PLASTIC STORAGE BAG

1

Fold in flap and roll top to eggs.

2

Place each pair back in the egg carton.

Bury in horse feed.

Then, holding one egg, twist the other until the bag is twisted tightly between the two. Now each egg is tightly wrapped in its own plastic compartment.

3

4 If eggs become broken they are still usable and each pair is in a separate plastic bag.

WEIGHING UP THE LOAD

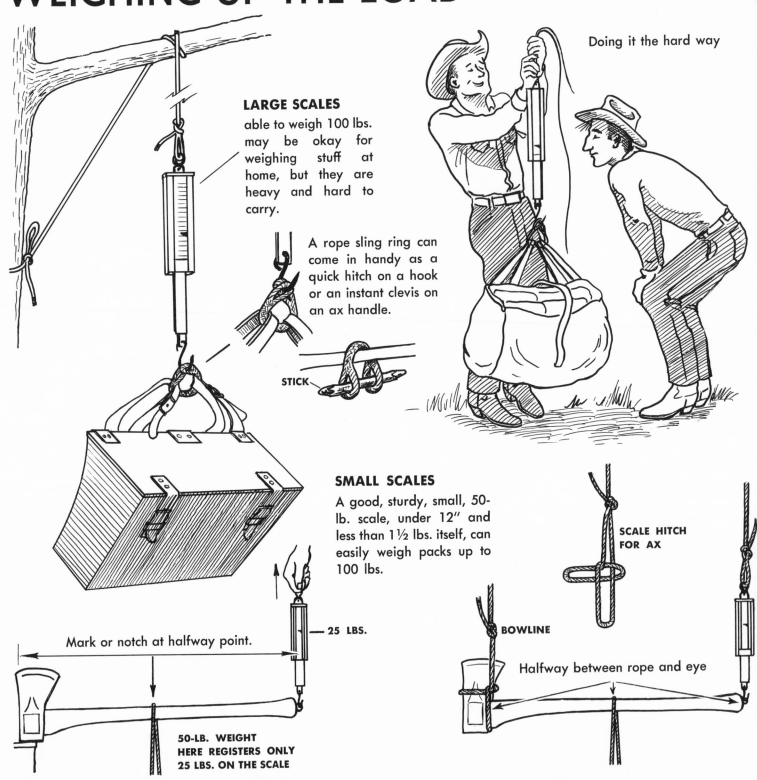

Doing it the hard way

LARGE SCALES

able to weigh 100 lbs. may be okay for weighing stuff at home, but they are heavy and hard to carry.

A rope sling ring can come in handy as a quick hitch on a hook or an instant clevis on an ax handle.

STICK

SMALL SCALES

A good, sturdy, small, 50-lb. scale, under 12" and less than 1½ lbs. itself, can easily weigh packs up to 100 lbs.

25 LBS.

Mark or notch at halfway point.

50-LB. WEIGHT HERE REGISTERS ONLY 25 LBS. ON THE SCALE

SCALE HITCH FOR AX

BOWLINE

Halfway between rope and eye

PACKING THE PACKER'S SADDLE

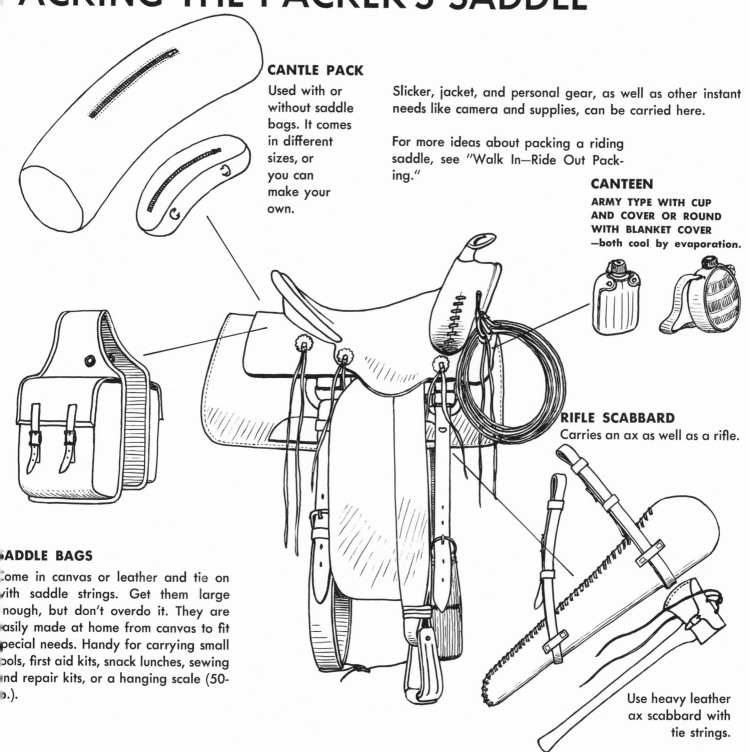

CANTLE PACK

Used with or without saddle bags. It comes in different sizes, or you can make your own.

Slicker, jacket, and personal gear, as well as other instant needs like camera and supplies, can be carried here.

For more ideas about packing a riding saddle, see "Walk In—Ride Out Packing."

CANTEEN

ARMY TYPE WITH CUP AND COVER OR ROUND WITH BLANKET COVER —both cool by evaporation.

RIFLE SCABBARD

Carries an ax as well as a rifle.

Use heavy leather ax scabbard with tie strings.

SADDLE BAGS

Come in canvas or leather and tie on with saddle strings. Get them large enough, but don't overdo it. They are easily made at home from canvas to fit special needs. Handy for carrying small tools, first aid kits, snack lunches, sewing and repair kits, or a hanging scale (50-lb.).

FIRST AID KITS FOR HORSE AND RIDER

Any first aid kit for horses should include most of these items. You should also be able to add your own needs.

FOR HORSE

If you are trained in horse medicine you will undoubtedly have a much longer list. The average rider is not trained sufficiently to administer drugs or to sew up a wound and should learn from a veterinarian how to use first aid properly but leave the doctoring to him.

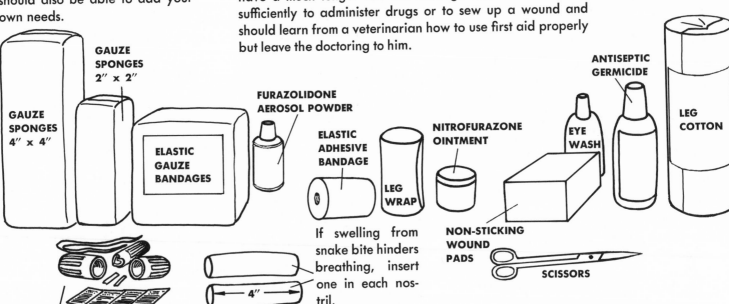

GAUZE SPONGES 2″ x 2″

GAUZE SPONGES 4″ x 4″

ELASTIC GAUZE BANDAGES

FURAZOLIDONE AEROSOL POWDER

ELASTIC ADHESIVE BANDAGE

LEG WRAP

NITROFURAZONE OINTMENT

ANTISEPTIC GERMICIDE

EYE WASH

LEG COTTON

NON-STICKING WOUND PADS

SCISSORS

SNAKE BITE KITS (SAME AS FOR RIDER)

If swelling from snake bite hinders breathing, insert one in each nostril.

4″

2 PIECES SMALL GARDEN HOSE

First aid kit for riders should include the following items. You will probably want to include some other items you personally prefer.

Soft burn ointment

Smelling salts

Snake bite kits

Merthiolate or iodine

Clean & treat pads

Aspirin

Mild soap

Butterfly closures (small, medium, large)

Cotton swabs

Boric acid

Adhesive tape

Alcohol swabs

Tourniquet

FOR RIDER

You may want to take insect repellent for relief from annoying insects. For obvious reasons *do not* carry with first aid or food items.

1″ adhesive compress

2″ bandage compress

3″ bandage compress

4″ bandage compress

3″ x 3″ plain gauze pads

Gauze roller bandage

Eye dressing packet

Plain absorbent gauze, ½ sq. yd.

Plain absorbent gauze, 24″ x 72″

Triangular bandage

Scissors

Tweezers

For horse

FIRST AID

For rider

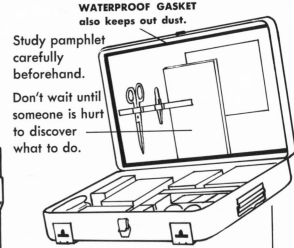

WATERPROOF GASKET also keeps out dust.

Study pamphlet carefully beforehand.

Don't wait until someone is hurt to discover what to do.

Portable industrial first aid cabinets like th will fit nicely in a saddle bag. The sturd metal case will protect items from breakag and dampness.

A special pair of first aid saddle bags mak needed items readily accessible.

SADDLING THE PACK HORSE

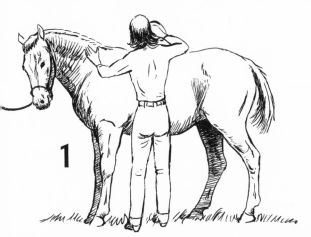

is as important to groom a pack horse as any other efore saddling.

se a good thick pad, such as quilted jute or hair-filled, r a special pack pad made of poly foam. Better yet, se one of the artificial fleece pack saddle pads.

OR EASY HANDLING PLACE HARNESS ON SADDLE.

Lay blanket on horse's back a few inches up and slide it back into position to keep hair lying naturally.

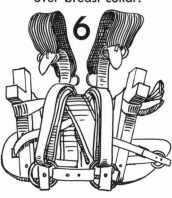

5 Then fold breast collar and connecting straps on top of breeching.

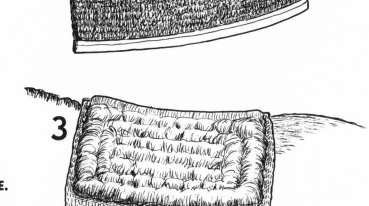

4

irst fold breeching and connecting traps; lay on top of saddle between orks.

Next fold latigos over breast collar.

6

Fold billets forward over saddle. Then fold cinches back. Saddle is now ready to be put on.

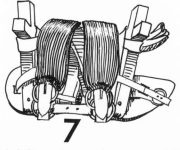

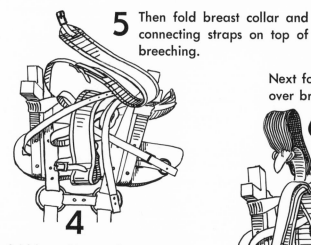

SADDLING THE PACK HORSE

1 Place pack saddle far enough up on withers so that front cinch will rest comfortably just back of the front legs.

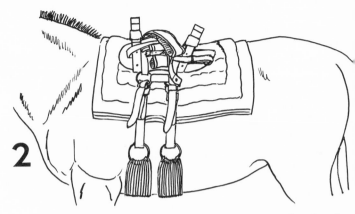

2 Start with front cinch—tie latigos snug. Don't take them up too tight, you'll tighten them later before loading.

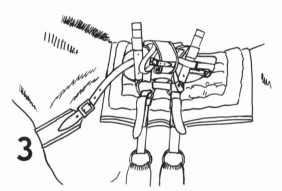

3 Next fasten breast collar by taking out slack. It shouldn't be tight: its only function is to prevent the saddle from slipping back.

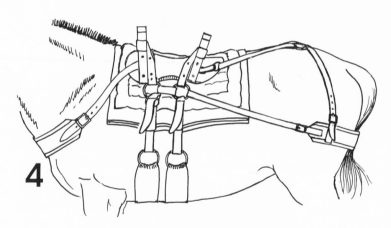

4 Then place and adjust the breeching.

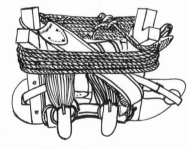

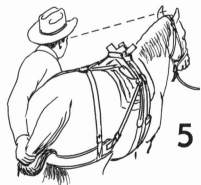

5 Unless you and your horse have a very good relationship, when removing his tail from under the breeching stand with your right side touching his left flank; his muscles will telegraph any intention to kick. Also watch his ears for a sign. Run your hand down over his rump and pull out the tail while talking to him, assuring him that everything is all right.

While unsaddling, harness is once more folded neatly on the saddle. After removing it from the horse, fold lash cinch, hook ring over a buck, and wrap rope around the bucks and tie off.

PREPARING THE DECKER FOR REMOVAL

To store sling rope on saddle, double rope and pull forward through back hoop.

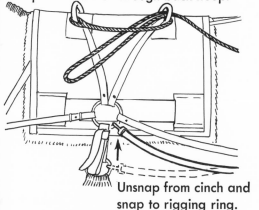

Unsnap from cinch and snap to rigging ring.

Coil remaining rope and tie coil to horizontal.

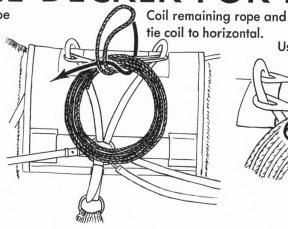

Use doubled rope as shown here.

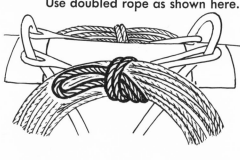

Now bring harness from the rear until hip pad is forward as far as possible. Lay breeching behind it.

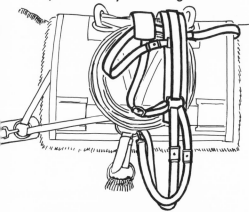

Next unsnap breast collar at left end. Fold back as far as it will go. Re-snap left end.

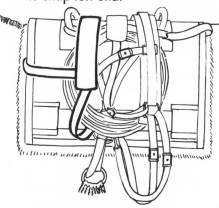

Then untie cinch. Bring it over saddle. Pass ring under hip strap. Thread latigo up through ring.

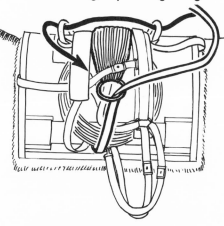

Thread latigo forward through hoops. Fold end back. Slip doubled end through cinch ring.

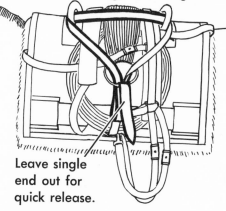

Leave single end out for quick release.

Lash and cinch can also be packed on a decker to keep them together until needed.

Run lash cinch through hoops; hook underneath in eye splice.

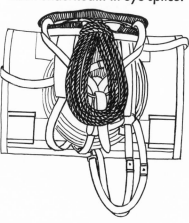

LOADING THE PACK HORSE

HOW TO FIGURE A LOAD

1

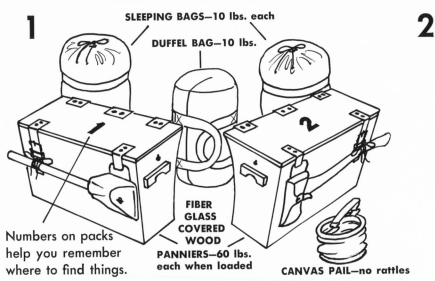

SLEEPING BAGS—10 lbs. each

DUFFEL BAG—10 lbs.

FIBER GLASS COVERED WOOD PANNIERS—60 lbs. each when loaded

CANVAS PAIL—no rattles

Numbers on packs help you remember where to find things.

If load is to be 150 lbs., start with net weight of gear such as sleeping bags, empty panniers, duffel bag, and tools (ax, shovel, pail), then add grain, groceries, and odds and ends to bring weight up to 150 lbs., distributing weight evenly on both sides. Ax, shovel, and pail are required by law for wilderness travel.

NOW CINCH TIGHT AND YOU ARE READY TO START LOADING.

2

Off pannier goes on first, then the near one. Next bedrolls, then duffel bag.

GLOVES

GLOVES

Each packer hooks the straps as pannier on opposite side is lifted into place.

SECURE TOP OF LOAD.

3

STRAPS

ROPE BUCKLE

Rope can take the place of straps.

HALF HITCH   QUICK RELEASE KNOT
HALF HITCH
HONDA KNOT OR EYE SPLICE

Make certain that bedrolls don't move by securing them to front and back bucks with "short ropes."

COVERING THE LOAD

4

One man—☼
See page 52.

Being careful not to overload, use anything from a small tarp to a tent as a cover, as long as it protects the cargo.

KEEP YOUR TOOLS AND FIRST AID KITS HANDY

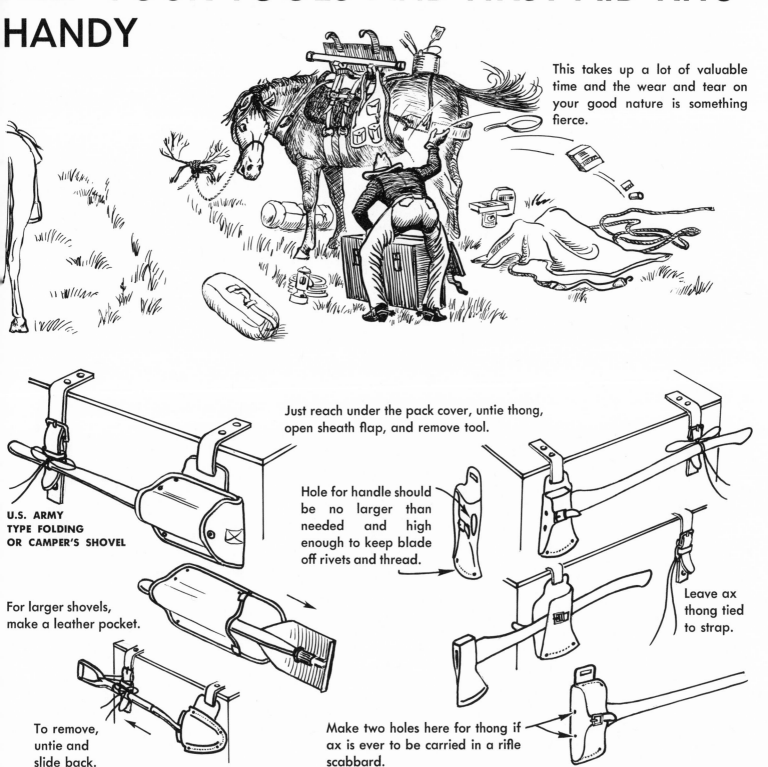

This takes up a lot of valuable time and the wear and tear on your good nature is something fierce.

Just reach under the pack cover, untie thong, open sheath flap, and remove tool.

U.S. ARMY TYPE FOLDING OR CAMPER'S SHOVEL

Hole for handle should be no larger than needed and high enough to keep blade off rivets and thread.

For larger shovels, make a leather pocket.

To remove, untie and slide back.

Leave ax thong tied to strap.

Make two holes here for thong if ax is ever to be carried in a rifle scabbard.

MAKING UP THE PACK STRING

The needs for a large pack train are figured in much the same way as for a small one. But since greater quantities are involved, some animals may carry a load that contains only one item.

The heavier packs go on the larger, stronger horses.

Grain or other unbreakable items may go to younger or less experienced animals.

Only the surefooted and trustworthy animals are assigned the very valuable or breakable items, especially if those horses are to be turned loose.

TIPS TO THE NEW PACKER

Never tie the lead fast to your saddle horn. Life can get a bit too exciting sometimes.

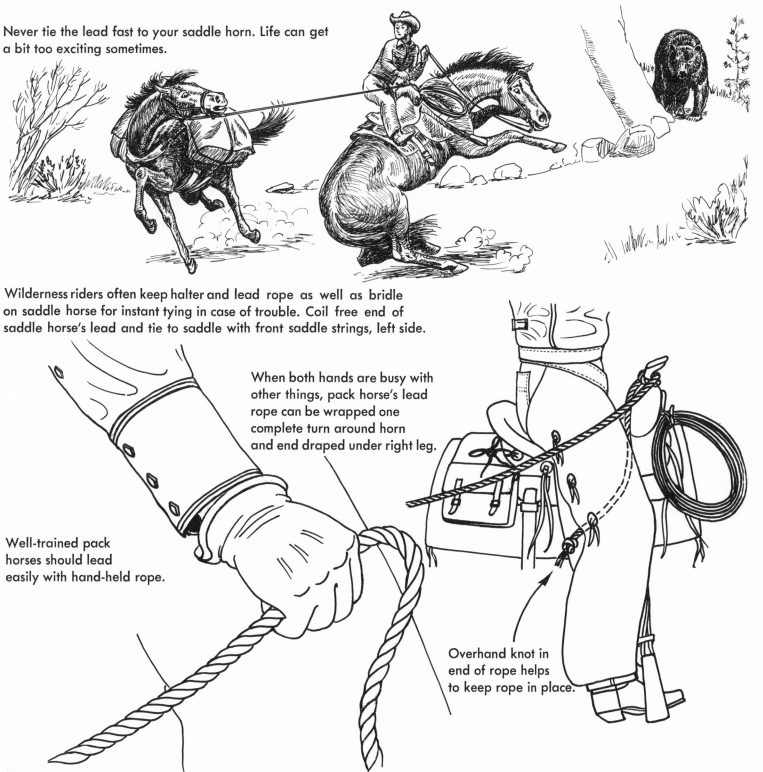

Wilderness riders often keep halter and lead rope as well as bridle on saddle horse for instant tying in case of trouble. Coil free end of saddle horse's lead and tie to saddle with front saddle strings, left side.

When both hands are busy with other things, pack horse's lead rope can be wrapped one complete turn around horn and end draped under right leg.

Well-trained pack horses should lead easily with hand-held rope.

Overhand knot in end of rope helps to keep rope in place.

ALONG THE TRAIL

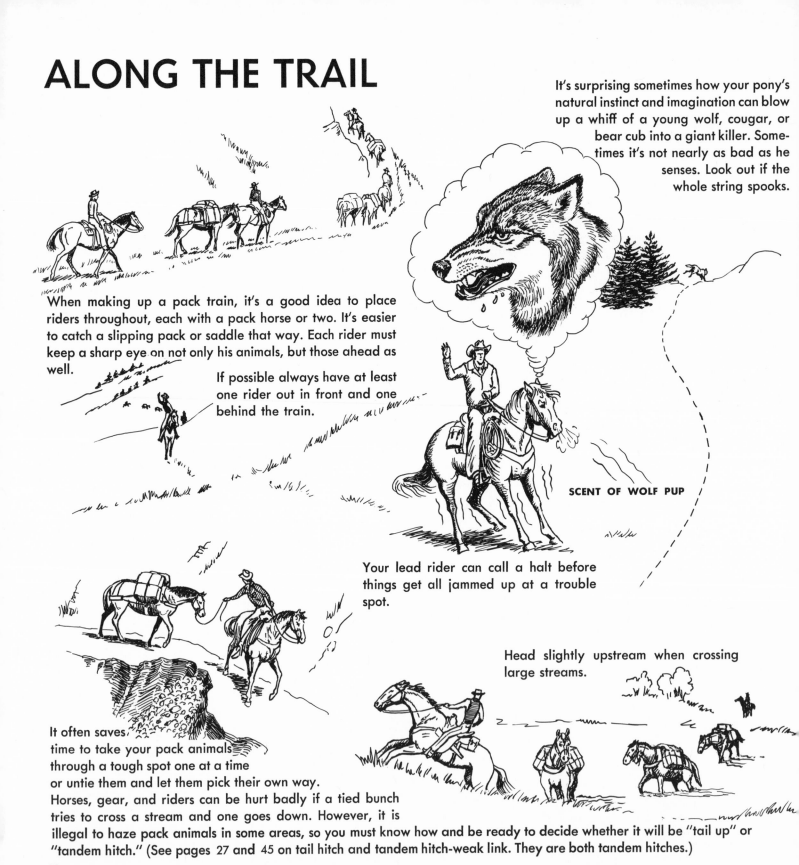

It's surprising sometimes how your pony's natural instinct and imagination can blow up a whiff of a young wolf, cougar, or bear cub into a giant killer. Sometimes it's not nearly as bad as he senses. Look out if the whole string spooks.

When making up a pack train, it's a good idea to place riders throughout, each with a pack horse or two. It's easier to catch a slipping pack or saddle that way. Each rider must keep a sharp eye on not only his animals, but those ahead as well.

If possible always have at least one rider out in front and one behind the train.

SCENT OF WOLF PUP

Your lead rider can call a halt before things get all jammed up at a trouble spot.

Head slightly upstream when crossing large streams.

It often saves time to take your pack animals through a tough spot one at a time or untie them and let them pick their own way.
Horses, gear, and riders can be hurt badly if a tied bunch tries to cross a stream and one goes down. However, it is illegal to haze pack animals in some areas, so you must know how and be ready to decide whether it will be "tail up" or "tandem hitch." (See pages 27 and 45 on tail hitch and tandem hitch-weak link. They are both tandem hitches.)

68

ALONG THE TRAIL

Make sure that all gear is in good shape and is clean. If a blanket falls to the ground shake it free of leaves, twigs, and any foreign matter and dry it after use. How would you feel with soggy underwear full of pine needles, sticks, and leaves? Your horse wouldn't like it either.

During any short stops, after you've been riding awhile, either tie your horse or hang on to him. When sweaty, horses love to roll, and being packed or saddled won't stop them from trying.

You could end up like this.

It's a good idea not to be treetop gazing on sharp turns or at any other time when your saddle horse could accidentally flip his tail over the lead rope.

ALONG THE TRAIL

A tiny spark can smolder for hours before bursting into flame.

If you have to smoke, save it for designated camping areas or stopovers in safe places.

A tinder-dry wilderness trail isn't smoker's country, buddy.

Never camp near enough to the trail to hinder other travelers.

Cutting corners may be tempting, but it doesn't take much trampling to kill the plants and start costly erosion damage, especially where ground cover is sparse. Stay on the hard trail.

A CAMP IS WHAT YOU MAKE IT

Picking a good camp site is half the battle. Look for sturdy trees for shelter on high ground, good running water for camp and horses, and lots of good grass.

If horses are thirsty let them drink a little on the way in if they aren't overheated. Unload at the edge of the camping area, tying horses to clean, live (safe) trees only. Stubs and brittle branches can put out a horse's eye—or yours.

After unsaddling, inspection for cuts, bruises, lost shoes, etc., and application of any needed medication, horses will have caught their breath. If you are carrying hay, you could give them some, then grain if you want, before turning them out on the grass. If you have no hay, feed them the grain *after* grazing. It's a good idea to get them used to coming for feed; it makes them easier to catch when needed.

Your horses have been working, so they have some grazing to catch up on. Take care of them and put them out on the grass as soon as possible. There is usually one—and like as not it's a mare—that the others will hang around. Bell and hobble or picket this one and some others who might range a bit more widely. Turn loose only those you can trust to stick around.

Water and feed the camp horse. Picket or tie him near camp for instant needs. (Two camp horses are company for each other.)

A CAMP IS WHAT YOU MAKE IT

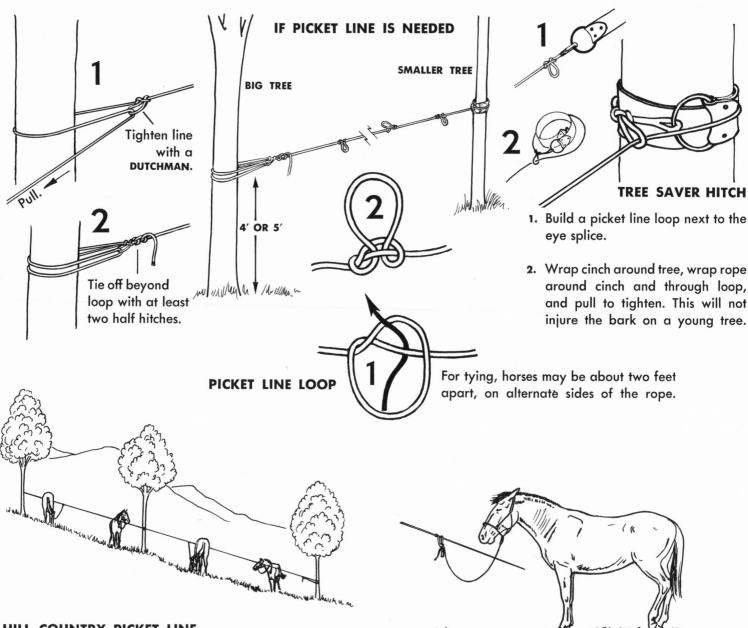

IF PICKET LINE IS NEEDED

1

Tighten line with a **DUTCHMAN.**

Pull.

2

Tie off beyond loop with at least two half hitches.

BIG TREE

SMALLER TREE

4' OR 5'

2

1

PICKET LINE LOOP

For tying, horses may be about two feet apart, on alternate sides of the rope.

1

2

TREE SAVER HITCH

1. Build a picket line loop next to the eye splice.

2. Wrap cinch around tree, wrap rope around cinch and through loop, and pull to tighten. This will not injure the bark on a young tree.

HILL COUNTRY PICKET LINE

Generally a picket line would be located on level ground but if it is necessary to put a picket line on a slope, it should run up and down hill so that each horse has a level place to stand. If horses must remain picketed for several days they should have plenty of hay and water, and manure must be removed frequently. Picket line should be moved to dry location as needed.

Tie ropes should be long enough to enable horse to eat hay from the ground and lie down comfortably, yet should not be long enough to allow the horse's feet to become entangled.

A CAMP IS WHAT YOU MAKE IT

A portion of salt block helps to keep horses near camp.

Hobble and bell the "boss mare" and one other horse. Loud bells make locating them easier.

Pick up all ropes not in use and keep them under shelter. This will make walking around camp at night less hazardous. Keep ropes dry. Wet ropes stretch as they dry out, resulting in loose packs on the trail.

Never tie a horse to an old dead snag. He could lose an eye or be cut and bruised from stubs or falling limbs.

A CAMP IS WHAT YOU MAKE IT

Two guards can keep each other awake.

If you are traveling in a "sensitive" area and prefer not to permit the horses to graze, build a rope corral and post a night guard. In this situation you'll have to pack a little more feed for the horses, but it saves the landscape.

CHORES

Many hands make light work. However some supervision is needed until everyone knows at a glance what should be done. Each pack group should have its trail and camp boss. Delegating work eliminates the chance of duplication and omissions and cuts down the time spent doing chores.

A CAMP IS WHAT YOU MAKE IT

Young and healthy trees offer shelter and shade for tents. Old trees may be more magnificent to look at, but a sudden storm with high winds could shower you with dry and deadly branches. The safest location is out in the open.

The base of a rock face may look like the perfect setting for a sleeping bag or tent. But pieces of rock loosened by weather or dislodged by man or beast at the top could end the pleasure of a place like that in seconds.

Given a choice it would be better to carry water a few more yards from a spring than to drink from a stream. Keep horse and latrine pollution well away from source of drinking water.

A nice flat valley floor isn't always the best place for a tent either. Stay on high ground to avoid runoff in case of rain.

A CAMP IS WHAT YOU MAKE IT

AN EASY-TO-BUILD SADDLE RACK

All that's needed for this are some of the short ropes you use to hang manteed hay on the sawbuck and a good sturdy *dead* pole. Don't cut live trees. This can also be used for a seat in camp or a latrine seat.

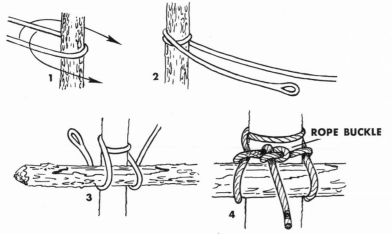

If one "short rope" isn't enough, use two. You would usually have them in sets of four anyway.

Tying ends of tarp together or to an object on the ground will keep tarp from blowing away. A little weight can help also.

CANVAS SHELTERS

Tarps have many uses besides being good pack covers on the trips in and out of camp. They can double for many things around the camp.

Of course with large groups or on a long stay, an extra tent for gear and supplies is best.

A CAMP IS WHAT YOU MAKE IT

CAMP FIRES

WHERE TO BUILD

ON SAND OR GRAVEL

Stones can be used for stove, but if wet, heat slowly.

WHERE NOT TO BUILD

NEVER ON FOREST FLOORS COVERED WITH HEAVY LEAF MOLD OR PINE NEEDLES

This material can smolder and burn for days, and fire can sometimes travel long distances in it.

ON CLAY, HARD PAN, OR OTHER NON-INFLAMMABLE GROUND

Remove dry grass and other burnables. Build your fire between wet or frozen logs. Don't cut live trees.

NEVER NEAR THE BASE OF A TREE OR WHERE DRY BRANCHES, BRUSH, OR DEAD GRASS CAN CATCH ON FIRE

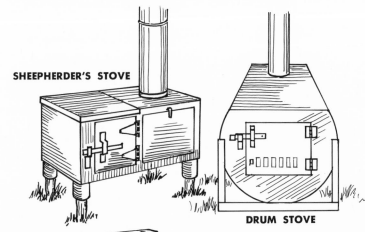

SHEEPHERDER'S STOVE

DRUM STOVE

GAS AND PROPANE STOVES

Small wood-burning stoves are nice for warming tents when it is cold. However, at popular sites wood may be scarce so take your gas or propane cook stove along.

Never build a roaring fire in a fireplace of wet or frozen stones. Some stones explode violently from heat.

A CAMP IS WHAT YOU MAKE IT

For short stops on the trail

MULTIPLE USES FOR EQUIPMENT SAVE TIME, WEIGHT, AND MONEY.

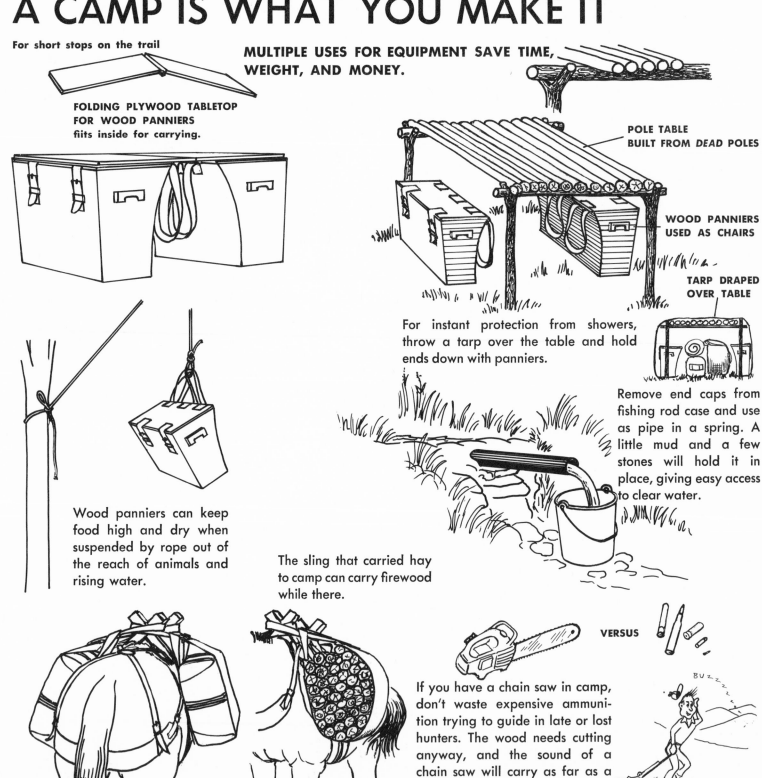

FOLDING PLYWOOD TABLETOP FOR WOOD PANNIERS fiits inside for carrying.

POLE TABLE BUILT FROM *DEAD* POLES

WOOD PANNIERS USED AS CHAIRS

TARP DRAPED OVER TABLE

For instant protection from showers, throw a tarp over the table and hold ends down with panniers.

Remove end caps from fishing rod case and use as pipe in a spring. A little mud and a few stones will hold it in place, giving easy access to clear water.

Wood panniers can keep food high and dry when suspended by rope out of the reach of animals and rising water.

The sling that carried hay to camp can carry firewood while there.

VERSUS

If you have a chain saw in camp, don't waste expensive ammunition trying to guide in late or lost hunters. The wood needs cutting anyway, and the sound of a chain saw will carry as far as a blast from "ol' Betsy."

BUZZZZ

78

WALK IN–RIDE OUT PACKING

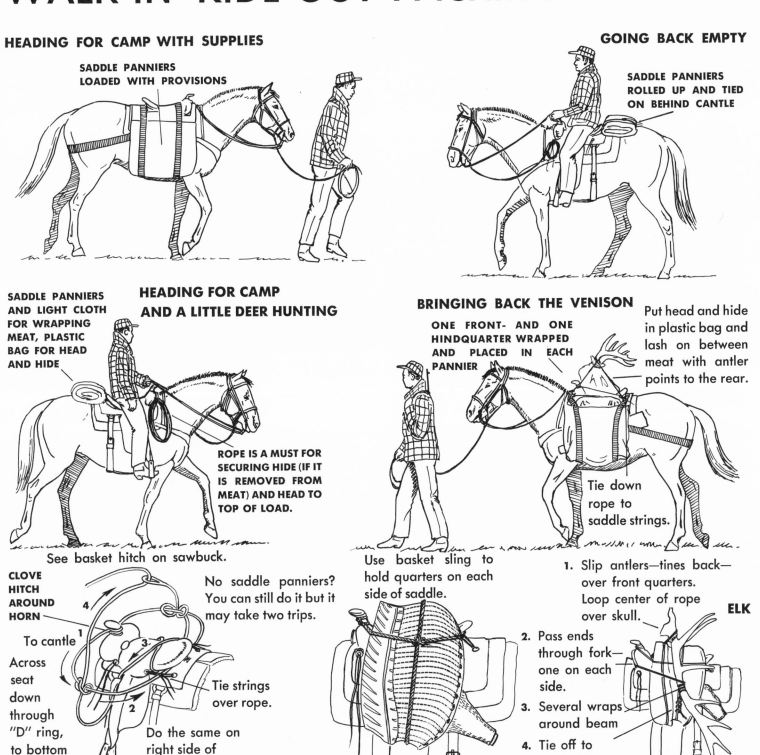

HEADING FOR CAMP WITH SUPPLIES

SADDLE PANNIERS LOADED WITH PROVISIONS

GOING BACK EMPTY

SADDLE PANNIERS ROLLED UP AND TIED ON BEHIND CANTLE

HEADING FOR CAMP AND A LITTLE DEER HUNTING

SADDLE PANNIERS AND LIGHT CLOTH FOR WRAPPING MEAT, PLASTIC BAG FOR HEAD AND HIDE

ROPE IS A MUST FOR SECURING HIDE (IF IT IS REMOVED FROM MEAT) AND HEAD TO TOP OF LOAD.

BRINGING BACK THE VENISON

ONE FRONT- AND ONE HINDQUARTER WRAPPED AND PLACED IN EACH PANNIER

Put head and hide in plastic bag and lash on between meat with antler points to the rear.

Tie down rope to saddle strings.

See basket hitch on sawbuck.

CLOVE HITCH AROUND HORN

To cantle

Across seat down through "D" ring, to bottom of sling and up.

Tie strings over rope.

Do the same on right side of saddle also.

No saddle panniers? You can still do it but it may take two trips.

Use basket sling to hold quarters on each side of saddle.

1. Slip antlers—tines back— over front quarters. Loop center of rope over skull.

2. Pass ends through fork— one on each side.

3. Several wraps around beam

4. Tie off to vertical sling rope.

ELK

PACK HORSES FOR BACKPACKERS

For the sturdy individual who likes to hike to his destination and stay awhile, a pack horse, mule, or burro to carry provisions may be the answer. But don't forget that your four-footed friend must eat and drink too. Plan your trip to water and grass and lots of it. That way he can carry more for you, since a large part of his needs will be waiting for him when he arrives.

LEAPFROG FISHING

Fisherman A fishes the stream to a predetermined pool where he meets fisherman B who went straight there with their pack horse. Horse grazes while B fishes the pool until A arrives. After a bite to eat A takes the horse and heads for another big pool and B makes his way to it along the stream, fishing as he goes.

BREAKING CAMP AND CLEANING UP

Reduce to ash all burnables. Then drench and bury. Drench again before covering with earth.

Smash all cans flat. Collect all bottles and load in panniers.

Make sure they are packed tightly so they won't rattle on the trip home.

Much time can be saved if all items that go on each horse are placed where the horse is to be tied.

Horses should be checked and groomed. Also check blankets and pads for mud, sticks, burrs, etc.

Latrines should be well covered with earth and stones to discourage animals from digging.

If you camped at a site frequented by campers, leave it neat for the next party.

If there were no signs of other campers, return the place as close to its natural appearance as possible before leaving. Scatter stones used to build fireplace, etc.

NOW BACK TO THE HOME CORRAL

Saddling and packing should be done quickly and horses moved out without unnecessary standing around.

It's every bit as important to be alert on the trip home as it was on the way in. Check lash ropes, packs, and horses to keep things moving smoothly. No sense in ruining a good trip at this point.

It's been a good outing. All went well and now you're back home. Your friendly four-legged transports are about all taken care of, but there is still one more chore to be done. The gear must be unpacked, cleaned, and stored where it can stay dry and be ready for next time.

TRAIL'S END

Don't spare the saddle soap and be sure to clean all the feed out of the panniers. Rub tools down with oil rag or a little "rig" grease to prevent rust. Once everything is spick-and-span you'll be all set for your next trip into the back country.

EASY-TO-MAKE AND EASY-TO-CARRY ITEMS

"JOHANNES" LEATHER PUNCH

A handy, lightweight, efficient leather punch can be made easily from a large nail. A three-flat-sided taper with 20° corners cuts holes in a variety of sizes. It can be resharpened on your ax hone.

TRANSFER YOUR INFANTRY CANTEEN TO THE CAVALRY.

A G.I. canteen with cup and cover is one of the handiest items you can carry. The metal variety can serve as a water bottle, tea kettle, cooking pot, cereal dish, and cup. If watercolor painting is your specialty, it can provide a supply of water and a cup for washing brushes. All that is needed for this canteen to ride nicely on a saddle are five strap loops of leather or webbing, riveted or sewn onto the cover, a strap, a ring, and a thong. The strap enables you to hook the canteen onto a ring or some other part of the saddle, and the thong ties it down so it doesn't bounce. If you have a favorite spot for carrying your canteen, a snap or ring can be attached to hook the strap in. Always hook the canteen on with the cover snaps toward the saddle so they won't be accidentally opened by branches or brush.

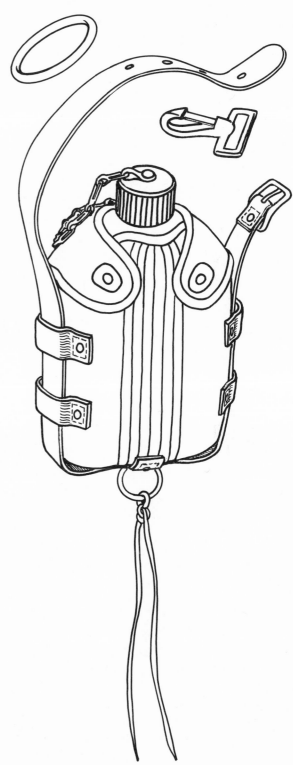

KEEP YOUR PAPER DRY!

A couple days' supply fits nicely into a plastic storage bag.

EASY-TO-MAKE AND EASY-TO-CARRY ITEMS

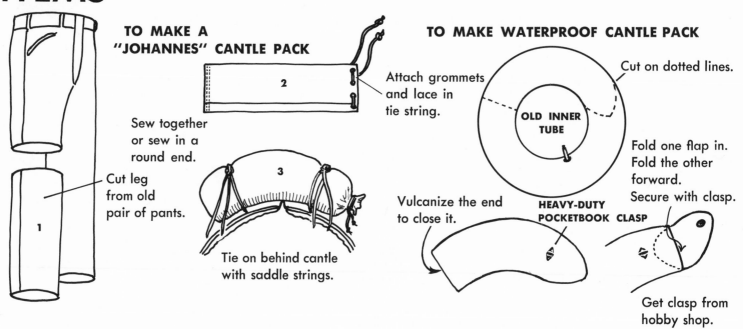

TO MAKE A "JOHANNES" CANTLE PACK

2

Sew together or sew in a round end.

Cut leg from old pair of pants.

1

3

Attach grommets and lace in tie string.

Tie on behind cantle with saddle strings.

TO MAKE WATERPROOF CANTLE PACK

Cut on dotted lines.

OLD INNER TUBE

Fold one flap in. Fold the other forward. Secure with clasp.

Vulcanize the end to close it.

HEAVY-DUTY POCKETBOOK CLASP

Get clasp from hobby shop.

"QUICKIE" MORRAL (FEED BAG)

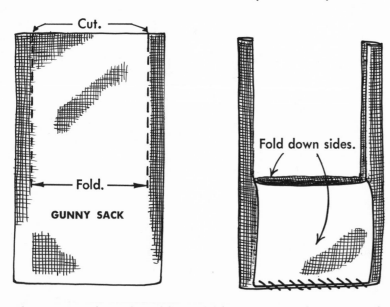

Cut.

Fold.

GUNNY SACK

Fold down sides.

After cutting along dotted lines, fold center flaps down on each side and sew with string to bottom. Adjust morral to fit horse and tie knot to keep it in place.

Lighter in weight and not as stiff as a regular nose bag, this can be carried easily and can be made on the spot for instant use.

DEAS FOR CARRYING ODDS AND ENDS

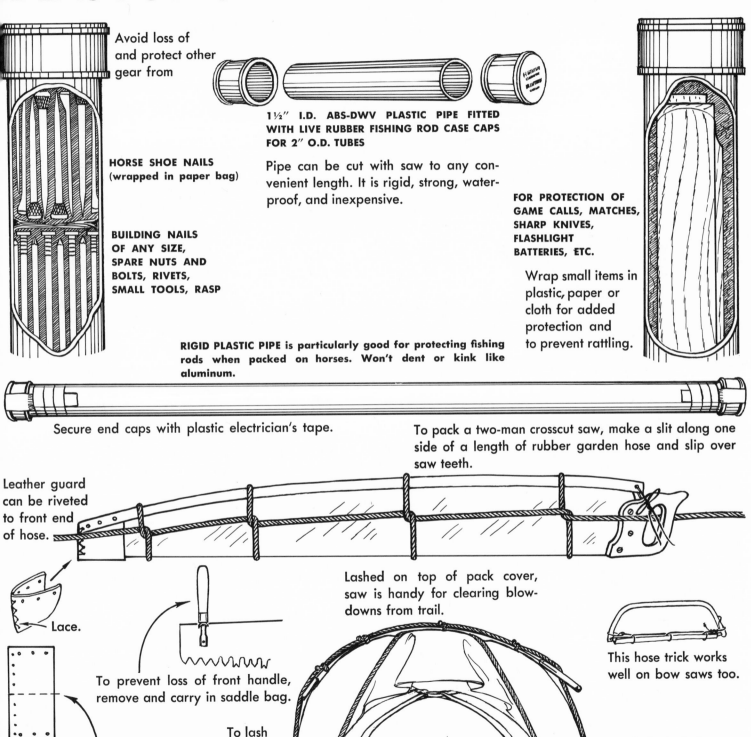

Avoid loss of and protect other gear from

HORSE SHOE NAILS (wrapped in paper bag)

BUILDING NAILS OF ANY SIZE, SPARE NUTS AND BOLTS, RIVETS, SMALL TOOLS, RASP

1½" I.D. ABS-DWV PLASTIC PIPE FITTED WITH LIVE RUBBER FISHING ROD CASE CAPS FOR 2" O.D. TUBES

Pipe can be cut with saw to any convenient length. It is rigid, strong, waterproof, and inexpensive.

FOR PROTECTION OF GAME CALLS, MATCHES, SHARP KNIVES, FLASHLIGHT BATTERIES, ETC.

Wrap small items in plastic, paper or cloth for added protection and to prevent rattling.

RIGID PLASTIC PIPE is particularly good for protecting fishing rods when packed on horses. Won't dent or kink like aluminum.

Secure end caps with plastic electrician's tape.

To pack a two-man crosscut saw, make a slit along one side of a length of rubber garden hose and slip over saw teeth.

Leather guard can be riveted to front end of hose.

Lace.

To prevent loss of front handle, remove and carry in saddle bag.

Lashed on top of pack cover, saw is handy for clearing blowdowns from trail.

This hose trick works well on bow saws too.

Fold leather here to make boot for end of saw.

To lash cinch hook

To lash cinch ring

A SLING OF MANY USES YOU CAN MAKE

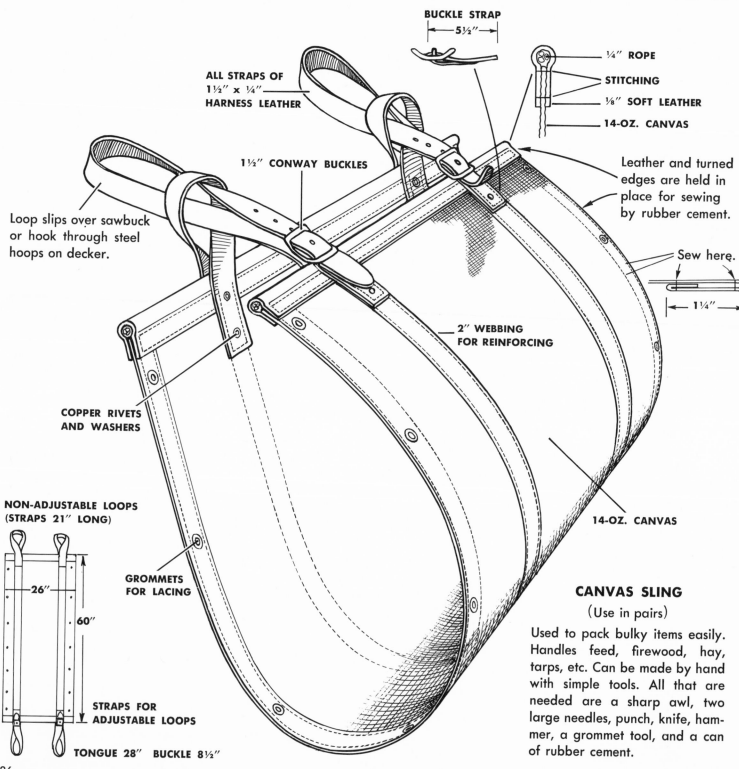

BUCKLE STRAP
5½"

¼" ROPE

STITCHING

⅛" SOFT LEATHER

14-OZ. CANVAS

ALL STRAPS OF
1½" x ¼"
HARNESS LEATHER

Leather and turned
edges are held in
place for sewing
by rubber cement.

1½" CONWAY BUCKLES

Sew here.

1¼"

Loop slips over sawbuck
or hook through steel
hoops on decker.

2" WEBBING
FOR REINFORCING

COPPER RIVETS
AND WASHERS

14-OZ. CANVAS

NON-ADJUSTABLE LOOPS
(STRAPS 21" LONG)

26"

60"

GROMMETS
FOR LACING

CANVAS SLING

(Use in pairs)

Used to pack bulky items easily.
Handles feed, firewood, hay,
tarps, etc. Can be made by hand
with simple tools. All that are
needed are a sharp awl, two
large needles, punch, knife, hammer, a grommet tool, and a can
of rubber cement.

STRAPS FOR
ADJUSTABLE LOOPS

TONGUE 28"   BUCKLE 8½"

STURDY, LIGHTWEIGHT, DO-IT-YOURSELF PANNIERS

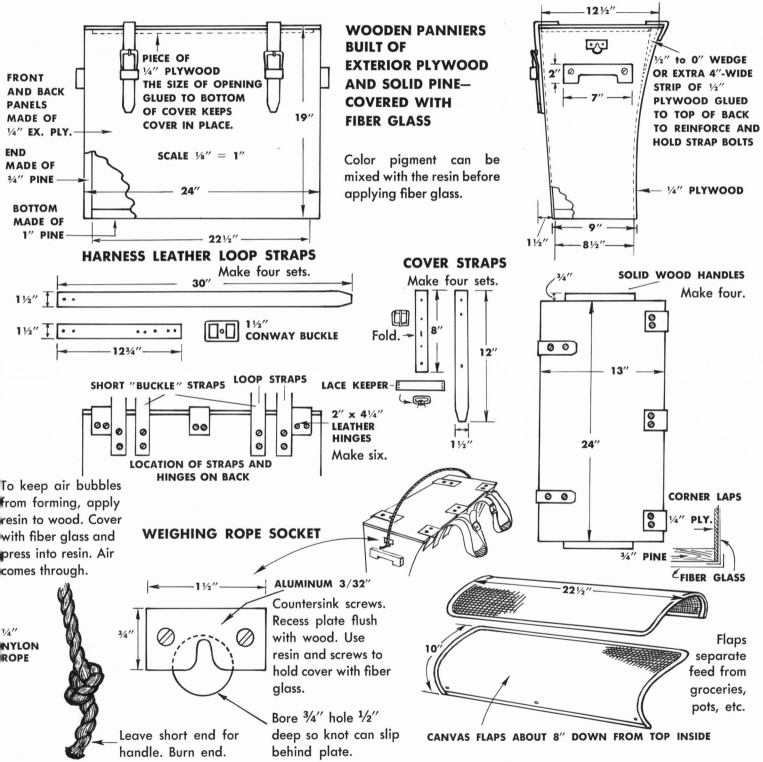

WOODEN PANNIERS
BUILT OF
EXTERIOR PLYWOOD
AND SOLID PINE—
COVERED WITH
FIBER GLASS

Color pigment can be mixed with the resin before applying fiber glass.

PIECE OF ¼" PLYWOOD THE SIZE OF OPENING GLUED TO BOTTOM OF COVER KEEPS COVER IN PLACE.

FRONT AND BACK PANELS MADE OF ¼" EX. PLY.

END MADE OF ¾" PINE

BOTTOM MADE OF 1" PINE

SCALE ⅛" = 1"

19"
24"
22½"

½" to 0" WEDGE OR EXTRA 4"-WIDE STRIP OF ½" PLYWOOD GLUED TO TOP OF BACK TO REINFORCE AND HOLD STRAP BOLTS

12½"
2"
7"
¼" PLYWOOD
9"
8½"
1½"

HARNESS LEATHER LOOP STRAPS
Make four sets.

30"
1½"
1½"
12¾"
1½" CONWAY BUCKLE

COVER STRAPS
Make four sets.

Fold. →
8"
12"
1½"

LACE KEEPER

SHORT "BUCKLE" STRAPS   LOOP STRAPS

2" x 4¼" LEATHER HINGES
Make six.

LOCATION OF STRAPS AND HINGES ON BACK

SOLID WOOD HANDLES
Make four.

¾"
13"
24"
¾" PINE

CORNER LAPS
¼" PLY.
FIBER GLASS

To keep air bubbles from forming, apply resin to wood. Cover with fiber glass and press into resin. Air comes through.

WEIGHING ROPE SOCKET

ALUMINUM 3/32"
Countersink screws. Recess plate flush with wood. Use resin and screws to hold cover with fiber glass.

Bore ¾" hole ½" deep so knot can slip behind plate.

1½"
¾"

¼" NYLON ROPE

Leave short end for handle. Burn end.

22½"
10"

Flaps separate feed from groceries, pots, etc.

CANVAS FLAPS ABOUT 8" DOWN FROM TOP INSIDE

DO-IT-YOURSELF PANNIERS

After studying the plans for the fiber glass covered wooden panniers shown here, you may want to build a set either like the ones in the diagram or to your own specifications. One thing to be particularly careful of is not to make them too large. Hard panniers that are too big can touch the horse's shoulders as he walks and can rub a sore on him in short order.

Each of the panniers shown here is large enough to carry a load that together with the weight of the pannier can reach 75 lbs. When packed to capacity, two panniers can weigh the 150 lbs. that an average horse can carry easily.

MATERIALS NEEDED

WOOD
1 sheet ¼" x 4' x 8' exterior plywood (from which fronts, backs, and lids are to be cut)
1 pine board ¾" x 12½" x 8' (from which ends are to be cut)
1 pine board 1" x 9" x 4' (from which the bottoms will be cut)

LEATHER
21' of 1½" harness leather (in whatever lengths you can get, to cut straps from with little or no waste)
33½" of 2" harness leather (for hinges and keepers)

HARDWARE
28 ⅜" x 1½" carriage bolts with nuts and washers (to bolt leather to pannier back)
28 ⅜" x 1" carriage bolts with nuts and washers (to bolt leather to lid and front)
4 1½" conway buckles (for loop straps)
4 1½" flank cinch buckles (for fastening down lids)
1 1½" x 3" x 1/16" aluminum sheet (from which to cut 4 plates for rope sockets)

FIBER GLASS AND EPOXY RESIN
3 yards of 60" 7.5 oz. fiber glass cloth
2 quarts resin (you won't need all of this for the fiber glass so use it to cement the two pieces of the top together and to join all wood joints)

CANVAS AND ROPE
1 20" x 22½" piece of canvas, almost any weight (for making two flaps)
1 3' length of ¼" nylon rope (for weighing rope)

PROCEDURE

The dimensions given below are for the panniers shown on page 87. If you design panniers to your own specifications you will need to adjust the measurements and the amount of materials required.

Step #1

Cut out all panels.

Ends: 8½" x 12½" x 19"   From ¾" pine

NOTE: Horizontal measurements for end panels will be ½" shorter than the overall outside measurements of the constructed box because front and back ¼" panels are nailed to the vertical edges giving the side dimensions the extra ½".

Fronts: 19" x 24"   Backs: 19" x 24"
From ¼" plywood   From ¼" plywood

Lids: 13" x 24"   Bottoms: 8½" x 22½"
From ¼" plywood   From 1" pine

Step #2

Glue and nail the lower edge (8½") of end panels against ends of bottom of each pannier.

Step #3

You now have two three-sided frames. Glue and nail the front and back panels to them.

Step #4

From leftovers of ¾" pine board or by gluing two thicknesses of ¼" plywood together, make two reinforcement pieces 22½" wide and 4" deep, wedge-shaped from ½" along the 22½" top to a knife edge at the bottom. Glue this along the top of the back panel on the inside, with the wide edge of the reinforcement up. The reinforcement should butt up against the end panels. This will strengthen the section where the bolts fasten the loop straps to the pannier. This is important, for all the weight is supported from this point.

Step #5

With a plane or file, level and smooth off the top edges of the box. From ¼" plywood, cut a piece 22½" x 12" to be attached to the bottom of the lid. Before attaching, however, make sure the piece fits nicely in the opening of the top of the box. Then locate it carefully on the bottom side of the lid and mark the outline. Make sure you have it right—there is no taking it apart once the glue is set. Now glue it to the lid and clamp or weight it until dry.

Step #6

To build the weighing rope socket, use a ¾" bit to bore a hole ½" deep about 2" or 2½" down from the top edge of the box on each end at the point where the box will balance. You can find the center of balance by picking up the box by the ends with thumb and forefinger until you find the spot where the box hangs level. After boring the hole locate a 1½" x ¾" aluminum plate over the hole as shown, mark the outline, and remove enough wood to allow the plate to be flush with the surface of the wood. Now shape the notch in the plate, bore and countersink the screw holes, glue the recess that will receive the plate, and fasten the plate to the wood with screws.

Step #7

To cover the panniers with fiber glass, cut the fiber glass for each panel 1" to 1½" larger on all sides than the panel itself.

Mix only the amount of resin and hardener needed to complete the panel being worked on. When the mixture starts to set, all unused portions are wasted. It is also a good idea to mix the color with the resin before adding the hardener, since adding the color requires a good deal of stirring. That way you will have all the time possible to work the cloth into the glue before it begins to set. While applying the cloth, all air must be forced out so that the cloth lies perfectly flat and smooth.

There are many colors to choose from; burnt sienna, for example, produces a saddle leather color which goes well with any horse gear. Ask about colors where you buy your epoxy.

To start the operation, it is best to cover the bottoms of the panniers first. This way the overlapping from all sides winds up on the bottom where it can't be seen, and the overlaps from the bottom which extend up the sides are covered. Ends are done next. Their overlaps are covered by front and back sheets leaving only the narrower ends to be worked on to get rid of rough edges. Sanding and more colored glue will blend them in nicely. When covering pannier lids, the fiber glass cloth may extend down over the front and side edges and only as far back as the back edge of the lid. If you are not skilled in this work it would be better to do only one side at a time and let it dry before going on.

Step #8
Make the handles.   7″ x 2″   From ¾″ pine

Drill holes for screws in the handles with a drill bit the full size of the screw. After the fiber glass is all glued on and dried and all exposed edges have been sanded smooth, drill part way into the end panel with a smaller-sized bit so the screws will start more easily. Apply resin to the back of the handle and screw holes and screw into place.

Step #9
Cut straps and hinges. Shape the ends.

Loop straps: 30″ x 1½″   12¾″ x 1½″
Cover straps: 8″ x 1½″   12″ x 1½″
Hinges: 2″ x 4¼″
Keepers: 1″ x 3″ (or slightly more)

Slice 2″ leather into two 1″ pieces, then cut out the keepers. If the ends of each keeper are to be joined by lacing with heavy thread, they should be either drilled or punched with a thin pointed awl. If they are to be riveted they must be cut longer so they will overlap enough to allow room for a rivet and then tapered on the ends so as not to be bulky. Keepers are held in place by the upper and lower pieces of the buckle strap between the two bolts that fasten the straps to the pannier's front panel. Buckle straps are folded with the finished side out to locate the center. Punch a hole large enough to receive the tongue of the buckle in the center. Now punch another hole about ⅜″ down the strap on the side which will be toward the outside, and with a sharp knife cut out the leather between the two holes to make a slot which will allow the buckle tongue to move out when buckling the lid down.

Now locate, mark, and drill all ⅜″ holes on lid and box for straps and hinges. Fit each strap or hinge to its particular set of holes, mark, and drill them. To bolt the leather to the wood, the bolt heads of the carriage bolts should be slotted to receive a screwdriver; a screwdriver is needed to keep the bolt from turning when tightening the nut. Slotting can be made easier by placing two blades in the hacksaw at the same time. All bolts, of course, go in from the outside and a washer is used under the nut on each one. Tighten until bolt head starts to dent the leather. Cut off extra threads and file smooth and flush with the nuts. When all leather is fastened to a pannier, run the lid straps through the buckles, pull up tight, and mark the underside where the tongue hole is to go and punch it. It should be a little tight to buckle at first for the leather will stretch. This way the lid will always be shut tight when buckled. The end of the strap should now slide snugly in the keeper.

Step #10

The two canvas flaps, 10″ x 22½″, should have bound edges to prevent unraveling. They are fastened on the inside of the panniers, one to the back panel, another to the front panel, about 8″ down from the top. Coat 1″ along the 22½″ side with glue and press it against the wood. Hold it there with short staples from a staple gun. Later remove the staples. The flaps overlap each other the full width of the box and are used to separate and stabilize cargo. See page 55.

Step #11

The last thing to be done is to make a weighing rope. Tie an overhand knot 1″ from the end of a ¼″ nylon rope. Hook this in one of the weighing rope sockets and pull tight. Now pull the rope over the lid to the socket on the other end of the pannier. Allow about 1½″ (not more than 2″) of slack above the lid. Tie another overhand knot to fit in the second socket and cut the rope 1″ beyond that knot. The 1″ of rope at either end is used to pull the knot back out of the socket when removing the rope. To prevent these ends from unraveling, touch each with a lighted match to fuse the strands solidly together. See page 58 for weighing instructions.

HAVE YOU TRIED THESE?

THE LATEST THING IN HORSE LUGGAGE

Strong, lightweight, plastic panniers now on the market come with a choice of nylon or leather rigging. They adapt equally well to sawbuck and decker saddles. Some also have water containers which fit inside them without wasted space. Also available are form-fitting insulated liners for carrying ice and frozen food.

HOW TO PACK A FLY ROD

Carrying a fly rod on a pack horse in a manner that will enable the rod to arrive at its destination in its original number of pieces is a problem that has had fishermen scratching their heads for years. However, since the invention of rigid PVC water pipe, especially the heavy wall type, a very sturdy rod case can be fashioned at home by cutting it to an appropriate length and fitting the ends with plugs or caps. This will save your fancy aluminum case for less strenuous transportation. Slip the plastic case under the knot at the top of a squaw hitch over a soft top pack. Here it can snuggle in. Use the extra rope at the end of the lash to tie two half hitches in front of the squaw hitch knot and two more behind it. The case is now as safe as it can be on a horse. On top of the pack it is out of the way and lower than the rider on the horse ahead.

Never, and I do mean *never*, tie a rod case on the side of a pack where it can get caught on a tree or other obstacle.

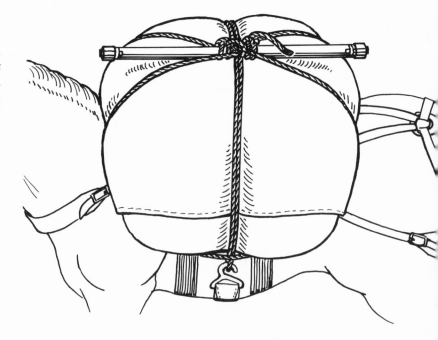

IT HELPS TO BE INVENTIVE

FIRST AID FOR AGING POLY FLEECE PACK PADS

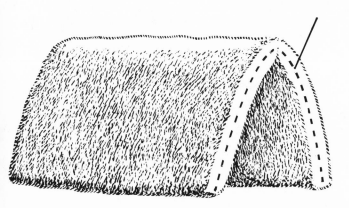

Is your poly fleece pad hard to wash? Is the cushioning material in it worn out? If so, there is a simple way to handle that.

Slit both sides of the end of the pad cover, as shown by the broken line on the diagram, and remove the inner pads. If they are starting to deteriorate, discard them.

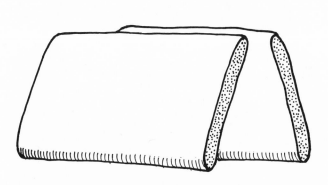

Good replacement material is available in various sizes and thicknesses at any upholstery shop.

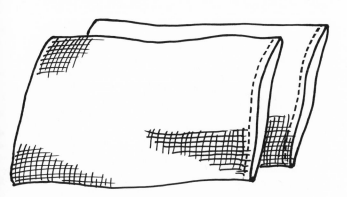

Lightweight slipcovers may be needed to make it easy to slide the cushion material in and out of the fleece cover.

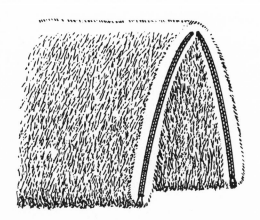

Zippers should be installed in both sides, and they should zip closed by pulling down, not up. This will keep them from opening while in use.

Remodeled in this way, the fleece cover and the slipcovers can be removed and washed and dried in a washing machine and dryer. In camp they can be taken apart to dry out faster.

TEACHING A HORSE-PACKING CLASS

An individual can easily learn one or more ways to pack a horse by merely referring to this book. However, teaching groups of people to be packers requires several instructors teaching separate operations simultaneously, to accomplish the most in the shortest time.

Horse Packing in Pictures originally came about as a textbook for a riding school which included horse packing and trail riding in its teaching curriculum. The first edition has been popular as a guide for this sport all over the United States and in countries around the world. Therefore it seems fitting to include one of our most successful packing-class techniques.

The following method proved to be most helpful in teaching packing to 4-H groups and other groups with fairly large numbers of students and limited time.

When planning a class it is important to weigh the number of students against the number of operations to be taught. Too many students in a class can lead to boredom while students wait their turn.

It is also best to start off with the saddling of the pack horse, followed by a step-by-step introduction to the various types of equipment and the uses of each.

For this it is best to set up stations for two or three different saddling procedures, including the sawbuck pack saddle, the decker pack saddle, and a Western riding saddle.

Each of these stations involves a horse and should include the following steps:

Step #1
Preparing the saddle: How to fold the harness on the saddle so it can be handled easily.

Step #2
Grooming the horse and placing the saddle pad.

Step #3
Saddling procedure.

With this accomplished, horses at all stations are ready and waiting for the placing of the panniers and whatever else is to go on. At this point each station can be involved with a different type of hitch or sling.

Each group learns the uses of different panniers and the hitches or slings best suited to them. When learning to attach panniers to a pack saddle, hard panniers and pack boxes need not have anything in them. However, soft canvas panniers must be stuffed with some light material to hold their shape. Even bales of hay can serve to teach how to use slings or "short ropes." A later station will be devoted to filling the panniers.

For the first lessons, the groups remain at the stations where they learn to saddle up. For the next lesson each group moves to the next station. The group at A moves to B, where they learn what is taught there. The group at B goes to C and so on, until all stations have been covered. Of course the last group moves to A. This continues until all students have completed all lessons.

Loaded panniers are rather heavy. Loading them on a horse is easier if the packers work in pairs. Consequently, it helps to teach the students in pairs. The first pair is taught by the instructor; then the first pair teaches the second under the watchful eye of the instructor. This is repeated until everyone at the station knows the procedure. The last pair can then demonstrate to the entire group, explaining each step as they go. One must concentrate when teaching, especially when questions must be answered, and the extra concentration and repetition works magic on students' memories. It also helps to command the attention of the entire group throughout the lesson.

We often play a game to sharpen the skills of students once they can successfully pack a horse. Choose two pairs of students with horses and equipment. Each pair competes against the other to see which can pack their horse best in the least amount of time.

The most interesting of these contests are the competitions between pairs of girls and boys. I will leave it to you to discover which pair usually wins.

Still another exercise simulates packing in the dark, accomplished by blindfolding the packers. This teaches students the importance of working together and always taking care of equipment so it can be located in the dark without having to hunt for it.

Training like this is especially important, for one never knows when an emergency may arise that would make it necessary to move out in the middle of the night. The following illustrates an example of how one can convert from sight to feel in the dark:

PROBLEM

Fastening a sling rope to the front buck of a sawbuck saddle necessitates building the required clove hitch in the center of the rope. How do you find the center?

SOLUTION

Grasp both ends of the rope in one hand and start pulling both strands through the other hand. When you run out of rope you have the center. See page 33 for a simple way to produce a clove hitch. This can be done very easily in the dark.

Once the packing lessons have been completed and students know the uses of ropes in packing, stations can be set up to devote time to building one's own set of ropes, making items of equipment, first aid for horse and rider, loading supplies into panniers, weighing panniers, setting up tents, cooking over outdoor fires, hobbling and picketing horses, and other related tasks.

Time spent in learning the skills necessary for a successful pack trip will not be wasted.

One very important operation is the planning and handling of food supplies and their placement in the panniers. Things you will need first should not be packed on the bottom.

If your pack trip is primarily for fishing, hunting, or other time-consuming activity, you will not want to spend unnecessary time making meals. Packing supplies in bags so they can fit into pots and pans can conserve space as supplies are depleted. Labeling supplies saves time and smoothes out the process of their use along the trail.

Snack lunches requiring no cooking can be bagged and labeled for particular meals or people if certain dietary requirements are called for.

If a camp is to be set up for a prolonged stay, kitchen supplies are usually packed in special pack boxes. The loading of kitchen supplies should be supervised by the person or persons who will do the cooking.

Organization eliminates confusion, saves time, and makes a packer's life much happier.